CW01630643

Roger Fry, Arthur Waley and Goldsworthy Dickinson:

The Cambridge Trio and the Discussion of the Modernity of Chinese Art in England

Hongyi Yang

Cam Rivers Publishing

First English Edition Published in Great Britain

By CAM RIVERS PUBLISHING LTD 2024
33 Trumpington Street
Cambridge CB2 1QY

ROGER FRY, ARTHUR WALEY AND GOLDSWORTHY DICKINSON:
THE CAMBRIDGE TRIO AND THE DISCUSSION OF THE MODERNITY OF CHINESE ART IN ENGLAND

Author: Hongyi Yang

Honorary Editor: Professor Alan Macfarlane FBA
Editor-in-Chief: WANG Zilan
Editors: WANG Zilan, QIN Yuchen

Cover Design: GE Dalong (MUYE)
Design and Typeset: QIN Yubin(MUYE)

Copyright of the Content © The Authors
Copyright of the Graphic Design © Cam Rivers Publishing

The publishing of this book is supported by
the Vanishing Worlds Foundation, U.K.
B&R Book Program

Cam Rivers ® logo is trademark and copyright © 2023 Cam Rivers Publishing Ltd. All right reserved. No part of this publication may be reproduced, stored in a retrieval system, or transmitted in any form or by any means, electronic, mechanical, photocopying, recording or otherwise, without prior permission of the copyright owner.

A CIP Catalogue of this book is available from the British Library

ISBN: 978-1-916858-05-3

Contact: press@cambridgerivers.com
www.cambridgerivers.com

ACKNOWLEDGEMENTS

I would like to express my gratitude to my MPhil supervisor Professor Jean Michel Massing, whose suggestions and guidance led to the conception of the topic – Roger Fry, Arthur Waley & Goldsworthy Dickinson: The Cambridge Trio and the Discussion of the Modernity of Chinese Art in England. Not only did he never tire of answering my seemingly infinite number of questions but also inspired me to expand my academic horizon.

I am grateful for the help of King's College Archives and Patricia McGuire, and for the support of the Apelles Art History Fund. My appreciation extends to all members of the University of Cambridge who supported me throughout my studies, many of whom I am now fortunate to consider friends.

Last but not least, I want to thank my family, especially my mother Beiqiong Xu for continuously standing behind me and giving me the courage and confidence to pursue my passions.

Preface I

The romantic poet and writer Xu Zhimo (徐志摩) (1897 – 1931) was an associate member for 18 months at King's College, Cambridge in the early 1920s. While he was there he met artists, intellectuals and writers of the Bloomsbury Group, including John Maynard Keynes, Bursar of the College, and wrote there his famous poem Zaibie Kangqiao (再别康橋), 'Taking leave of Cambridge again', starting with the following verses:

> "Softly I am leaving,
> Just as gently as I came;
> I gently wave goodbye
> To the clouds in the western sky".

In the early 1920s, John Maynard Keynes was a Fellow as well as bursar of King's College; he was both an economist and a philosopher but also a patron of the arts, an art collector and a key figure within the Bloomsbury Group. Goldsworthy Lowes Dickinson (1862 – 1932), too, was a philosopher and political thinker who became a Fellow of King's College in 1887 and was also part of the Bloomsbury set. In King's College, he taught history and politics. He became a close friend of the much younger Roger Fry (1866 – 1934), during the latter's last year of study at Cambridge (1887–1888). The orientalist Arthur David Waley (1889 – 1966) studied Classics at King's from 1907 to 1910; he was appointed Assistant Keeper of Oriental Prints and Manuscripts at the British Museum in 1913, where he worked until 1929; he is best known however for his writings and his translations of Chinese and Japanese poetry. He too was close to the Bloomsbury set. These three scholars were all important intermediaries for the reception of Chinese art in Cambridge.

In 2016-17, I supervised Hongyi Yang, of Clare College, for the MPhil in History of Art and Architecture at the Department of History of Art of the University of Cambridge. A graduate of Tsinghua University in Beijing, Hongyi exhibited the qualities we often associate with the best students from that university: intelligence, diligence, curiosity and a desire to make first rate contributions to the field. Hongyi became an excellent scholar and lecturer, and one of the very few students who completed the program with Distinction. When I met her, I was concerned at the beginning, as she was quiet and did not speak much during her supervisions. But then she produced her first assignment, which was an important contribution to the history of art, and gave oral accounts of her research with great authority. Using Chinese and European sources, her second long essay was on *Goddess of Mercy: The Influence of Chinese Export Ceramics and the Westernization of Dehua Guanyin*, under the influence of Indo-Portuguese ivories from Goa. The Chinese Bodhisattva Avalokiteshvara or Guanyin became the goddess of mercy for the Jesuits because of her iconographic similarity with the Virgin. Ceramic figures were exported to the West, but they are also found in the Chinese domestic sphere as the Westernization of Guanyin also blossomed in the domestic market. Hongyi's first Essay had given her a first insight into the 'Cambridge Trio': *Roger Fry: The Chinaman – Formalism and Chinese Art (*the title is based on Goldworthy Lowes Dickinson's *Letters from John Chinaman* of 1901). A painter and art critic, Fry, who never visited China nor had a first-hand exposure to its culture and language, integrated his interest in Chinese art within his Formalism. Fry mainly knew Chinese art through the activities of French dealers and his formalistic approach allowed him to interpret it without knowledge of its content, but he saw this as a compromise as the field at this time had no real scholarly basis in the West. So he contrasted an Italian mid-fourteenth century sculpture with an earlier Tang dynasty (618 – 907) rendering of Bhikshu. The modernity of Chinese art became apparent to him through his study of some linear and flat designs in Han (206 BC – AD 220) art as well as oriental landscape paintings. He saw it as an antithesis to the Western anthropocentric attitude in the Chinese interest in animals and plant forms leading to an "art of freedom and gaiety". The interest and subtlety of Fry's approach are noted by Hongyi, but also his shortcomings: "Relying on scarce Shang material and few reference objects, Fry failed to notice subtle differences in expressive forces. Unable to physically scrutinize both items concurrently, he instead relied on his memory, low quality photographs and on comparative objects he had never encountered." This reservation is followed by an account of Fry's collection; mainly modest pieces, most of them have never been properly assessed before. They offer "a precious art-historical record for the development of the modern eye", provide "a prism into Fry's formalism", and present "a vivid expression of the 'Bloomsbury taste'". Here as elsewhere, Hongyi corrected Fry's opinions by giving a proper modern assessment of the pieces based on her knowledge and experience with Chinese antiquities, another of her areas of excellence.

Based on her MPhil dissertation, the present book (*Roger Fry, Arthur Waley and Goldsworthy Dickinson: The Cambridge Trio and the Discussion of the Modernity of Chinese Art in England*) deals with the three figures mentioned above, all associated with King's College, Cambridge. They initiated art-historical debate about traditional Chinese art in the early decades of the twentieth century, reaching conclusions about the modernity, classic spirit, and accessibility of Chinese art through methodologies of formalist aesthetics, historical study, and sociological analysis. At a time when first-hand material was scarce, the Cambridge Trio's ground-breaking and visionary research was pivotal in changing Western perceptions of Chinese art, influencing studies of modern art, literature, and social politics in the West. Their approaches intertwined and corroborated, as did their shared personal lives. This book fills a void by examining in depth the writings of the Trio on Chinese art, during a transitional period that led to further future (re-)assessment of Chinese art and its history.

I was delighted to see Hongyi blossom in her career as an art historian and most recently as Deputy Director and Specialist for Old Master Paintings at Sotheby's, London, where she created more cross-cultural dialogues, although in a very different manner. As I came to know her as a friend in more recent years, I am constantly surprised by her curiosity and enthusiasm to learn, as well as her wide interests and knowledge of arts, music, literature, and languages.

Professor Jean Michel Massing
King's College,
University of Cambridge

Preface II

There were many outstanding scholars from King's College, the University of Cambridge by the end of 19th century and the beginning of 20th century, including the writer Edward Morgan Forster (1879 – 1970), computer scientist Alan Turing (1912 – 1954), English Poet Rupert Brooke (1887 – 1915) and the Chinese visiting scholar and poet XU Zhimo (1897 – 1931). The art critic Roger Fry (1866 – 1934), orientalist and sinologist Arthur Waley (1889 – 1966), and political scientist Goldsworthy Dickinson (1862 – 1932) were connected to arts of China in various ways but had been ignored by historians of Chinese art.

I have known Miss Yang for more than ten years, before she arrived in Cambridge to do her MPhil in History of Art and Architecture at Clare College in 2016. I have enjoyed our many conversations about art, culture, and society, and am glad to see her progress from being a bright art history student and good helper at the museum to an entrepreneurial young professional in the international art world. Entitled *Roger Fry, Arthur Waley and Goldsworthy Dickinson: The Cambridge Trio and the Discussion of the Modernity of Chinese Art in England*, the present book is based on her MPhil dissertation and examines how the Cambridge Trio reached the conclusion that Chinese art is modern, embodies the classic spirit, and is accessible to Western audiences from angles of formalist analysis, literature and historical research, as well as sociological study.

Early twentieth century was a period when China transformed from the imperial Qing dynasty to the Republic of China, and the whole world also experienced huge political turbulences, such as the trade and war conflicts between East and West. As pointed out in the book, the railway construction in China engaged foreign technicians, while events such as the Boxer Rebellion and Opium Wars led to an unexpectedly substantial outflow of Chinese material. The important Chinese art trade started in the late nineteenth century, resulting in an increased presence of Chinese art in European collections. Scholars including the Cambridge Trio were thus provided with an unprecedented opportunity to examine Chinese art up close, thanks to newly formed collections by collectors such as George Eumorfopoulos and Adolphe Stoclet, as well as objects brought back from Paul Pelliot's and Marc Aurel Stein's expeditions. It was a phase when "passions for fresh visual sensations were strong, offering wide possibilities for pure aesthetic criticism when contextual knowledge was lacking".

The book gives an informative review of how Chinese art study became a trend and how serious academic scrutiny of the subject was established in Europe in the early twentieth century, by which time Chinese objects finally came to be defined as 'Chinese art' as opposed to 'Oriental objects' in England. France spearheaded the study of Chinese art with the opening of the Musée Guimet and Musée Cernuschi in Paris in the late nineteenth century, but was soon overtaken by the United States, where the art historian Ernest Fenollosa "played a vital role". With this contextual knowledge in mind, readers learn that it was in America where Roger Fry was supposedly introduced to Chinese art by Matthew Prichard of the Boston Museum of Fine Arts in 1905. Goldsworthy Dickinson's interest in the topic was, however, "spawned by his inquiries into Chinese society". The other member of the Trio Arthur Waley approached Chinese art from a literary perspective and translated Chinese literature from its original source, having been prompted by Ezra Pound's second-hand translation from French and possibly inspired also by Raphael Petrucci's method involving philosophy and theology when approaching Chinese art history.

Having studied first-hand materials from the King's College Archive Centre, Cambridge, the author recreates the time when the Cambridge Trio met and influenced one another and developed their methodologies towards Chinese art and history. In this book, Miss Yang argues that although the Cambridge Trio's methodologies varied, their thought processes and analytical deductions were "intimately intertwined from the early days of their friendship, blossoming with their shared passion for China and its culture" while satisfying the "modernist taste". The Trio's scholarly contributions not only belong to "the indispensable repertoire" of Chinese art studies, but also impacted areas including modern art, literature and social politics. The present book is an important contribution to the historical research on the writings on Chinese art. The studies carried out by Roger Fry, Arthur Waley, and Goldsworthy Dickinson of King's College, the University of Cambridge had never been thoroughly examined before. This book's discussions fill the gap in Chinese art history research in the early twentieth century Britain.

Dr. James C. S. Lin
Senior Curator of Chinese Art
Fitzwilliam Museum
University of Cambridge

Introduction: Three Kingsmen and their Connections to China

This book is about three figures from King's College, Cambridge, who together initiated art-historical debate about Chinese art in England in the early decades of the twentieth century.

The Cambridge Trio, composed of Roger Fry, Arthur Waley and Goldsworthy Dickinson, believed that Chinese art was modern and accessible to Western audiences. With their personal and professional lives intertwined, the three men were able to reach congruent and corroborating conclusions about Chinese art through formalist aesthetics, historical study, and sociological analysis. Although studies of Roger Fry's criticism, Arthur Waley's translations, and Goldsworthy Dickinson's political work abound, little work has so far been published about their writings on Chinese art.

Through an examination of the trio's individual perceptions and approaches towards Chinese art as well as a juxtaposition of their methodologies and theories, this book argues for the existence of a highly-coherent intellectual structure shared by the Cambridge Trio. These three thinkers should be credited with changing the Western perception of Chinese art, a ground-breaking labour fostered and supported by King's College and the University of Cambridge.

Roger Eliot Fry (1866 – 1934)

Born into a Quaker family in Highgate, London, Fry attended Clifton College before winning a science exhibition[1] to King's College, Cambridge in 1884. After departing Cambridge in 1888, he abandoned natural sciences and attempted a career as a painter before turning to art criticism. Fry co-founded *The Burlington Magazine for Connoisseurs* in 1903 and the Omega

1 An exhibition at Cambridge is a financial award or grant to an individual student on grounds of merit.

Workshops in 1913. He briefly moved to the United States, taking up the position of curator of European paintings at the Metropolitan Museum of Art in 1906. Initially an advocate of the old masters and Italian Renaissance art, Fry became renowned for introducing French Post-Impressionism to the English public, as well as for his formalist approach to world art. A member of the Bloomsbury Group, he shared the set's aesthetics and sensitivities. Fry was elected Slade Professor of Fine Art at the University of Cambridge where he lectured from 1933 to 1934.[2]

Arthur David Waley (1889 – 1966)

Born in Tunbridge Wells on 19 August 1889, Waley attended Rugby School where he won an open scholarship to King's College, Cambridge. After obtaining a first in part one of the classics Tripos, he had to withdraw from his studies in 1910 due to diminishing sight in one eye.[3] Joining the British Museum in 1913 as Assistant Keeper of Oriental Prints and Drawings, he taught himself Chinese and Japanese. Waley is most remembered for his translations of Oriental literature and poetry.[4]

Dickinson, Goldsworthy Lowes (1862 – 1932)

Born in Langham Chambers, London, Dickinson attended Charterhouse School before entering King's College, Cambridge as an exhibitioner in 1881. After graduating in 1884 with a first-class classics degree, he won a Fellowship at King's College with his dissertation on Plotinus in 1887, and lectured on political

---

2 Fry's major publications on Chinese art include: 'Chinese Art', *Burlington Magazine Monographs*, London, 1925; *Transformations*, London, 1926; *Last Lectures*, Cambridge, 1939.

3 Cambridge undergraduate courses are assessed through examinations called Triposes, which need to be completed in order to qualify for the B.A. degree.

4 Waley's major publications on Chinese art include: *A Hundred and Seventy Chinese Poems*, London, 1918; *An Index of Chinese Artists Represented in the Sub-Department of Oriental Prints and Drawings in the British Museum*, London, 1922; *Zen Buddhism and its Relation to Art*, London, 1922; *An Introduction to the Study of Chinese Painting*, London, 1923; *A Catalogue of Paintings Recovered from Tun-Huang by Sir Aurel Stein, K.C.I.E*, London, 1931.

science at the College from 1896 to 1920. A pacifist and internationalist, Dickinson was one of England's first advocates of the idea of a 'League of Nations'.[5]

5 Dickinson's major publications on Chinese society include: *Letters from John Chinaman*, London, 1901; *An Essay on the Civilisations of India, China & Japan*, London, 1914.

CONTENTS

The Cambridge Trio: Roger Fry, Arthur Waley and Goldsworthy Dickinson

The University of Cambridge might seem an unlikely fountainhead for Western Europe's recognition of modernity in Chinese art, yet it is there that a trio of restless and ambitious Cambridge Englishmen set out to enhance cultural and artistic understanding of China, rejecting long-established stereotypes about China's backwardness and the division between East and West. At a time when some still considered Chinese people 'barbarians', the conclusions reached by these individuals, coupled with their ground-breaking theories and methodologies, mark a point of departure deserving of further investigation.[6]

Three members of King's College, Cambridge, played pivotal roles in discovering and reviving Chinese art in the West. Roger Fry, Arthur Waley and Goldsworthy Dickonson's triangular relations reveal as much about their lives as about the intellectual atmosphere nurtured at Cambridge. Approaching the topic of Chinese culture from visual, literary and societal perspectives, the Cambridge Trio saw a modernity in Chinese art which few in the West had theretofore noticed or dared to mark. Fry appreciated formal quality deprived of context, and argued that Chinese art delights and comforts despite its most exotic and antique nature, stipulating ancient profound interconnections between East and West.[7] In Fry's argument, the underlying affective power of Chinese visual art makes it comprehensible and modern to the Western viewer. Waley, on the other hand, insisted on understanding cultural and historical traditions through the lens of literature, particularly poetry, which he translated in the fashions of contemporary Europe. Meanwhile, Dickinson

6 G. Dickinson, 'Letters from John Chinaman', *Letters from John Chinaman and Other Essays*, London 1946, pp. 19, 43.

7 R. Fry, 'Chinese Bronzes at Messrs. Yamanaka's', *Nation and Athenaeum*, 1926, pp. 494-95; R. Fry, 'Review of *Ruins of Desert Cathay* by M. A. Stein', *The Burlington Magazine for Connoisseurs*, 21, 1912, p. 174. See also R. Fry, 'Chinese Art at the Whitechapel Gallery', *Athenaeum*, 3849, 1901, p. 165.

described Chinese poetry as 'most human',[8] representing life in a realist mode. For him art was part of the societal mechanism, and the humanity of Chinese society made its art modern. Seemingly disparate, their methods came into lively dialogue with one another in enduring relationships forged at Cambridge.

Of the Cambridge Trio, only Goldsworthy Dickinson ever visited China, and only after the completion of his major publication on the subject. Able to communicate with Chinese scholars only in writing, Arthur Waley 'felt so at home in T'ang China' that he rejected numerous invitations to visit the country as he could not bear its 'modern ugliness'.[9] Despite an invitation to talk about modern art by the Chinese poet Xu Zhimo, Roger Fry never managed to visit China.[10] Relying on formalism, an approach to art based on analysis of design and the constituent 'emotional' elements of 'line', 'mass' and 'colour', he was able to conjecture and theorize on different aspects of foreign art, laying the theoretical groundwork for the acceptance of abstraction.[11] For Dickinson, Chinese art provided a cultural refuge. His observations of Chinese society were deemed enlightening for presenting a contrasting perspective to many Victorian writings, although he was criticized for being 'over-confident' about a country he barely knew.[12] Nonetheless, his writings offered

---

8 G. Dickinson, 'An Essay on the Civilisations of India, China and Japan', *Letters from John Chinaman and Other Essays*, London 1946, p. 66.

9 'He Never Went to China – A Portrait of Arthur Waley', *The Listener 2 August 1979*, compiled and presented by F. Watson for Radio 3, King's College Archive, ADW 4/4, p. 139; I. Morris, 'Arthur Waley', *Encounter*, 12, 1966, p. 54.

10 P. Laurence, *Lily Briscoe's Chinese Eyes: Bloomsbury, Modernism, and China*, Columbia, SC 2003, p. 347.

11 R. Fry, 'An Essay in Aesthetics', *Vision and Design*, London, 1923, pp. 30-35; C. Reed, 'The Fry Collection at the Courtauld Institute Galleries', *The Burlington Magazine*, 132 (1052), 1990, pp. 766-67.

12 For examples of Victorian writing see *A Century of Travels in China: Critical Essays on Travel Writing from the 1840s to the 1940s*, ed. D. Kerr and J. Kuehn, Hong Kong 2007; for criticism, see J. Harding, 'Goldsworthy Lowes Dickinson and the King's College Mandarins', *The Cambridge Quarterly*, 2011, p. 31.

comfort to Chinese visitors, including Xu Zhimo.[13]

Although the University of Cambridge has been acknowledged for various academic achievements, its importance and influence in shaping the Western perception of Chinese art is often left unmentioned. Patricia Laurence's 2003 *Lily Briscoe's Chinese Eyes: Bloomsbury, Modernism, and China* could be considered the most relevant publication on the topic so far. Examining interconnections between the Bloomsbury Group in England and the Crescent Moon Group in China, she explores Chinese arts, principally literature, through the prism of British modernism. Whilst Fry's discussions of Chinese art, Dickinson's redefinitions of British 'civilization' in relation to China, and Waley's translations of Chinese literature are given due credit, the emphasis is placed on their respective relations to the Bloomsbury Group and contributions to British re-evaluation of Chinese literature and art. The Trio's pioneering work and wide-ranging methodology on the modernity of Chinese art deserve more detailed analysis and wider recognition.

13 I. Richards, 'The Chinese Renaissance', *Scrutiny*, 9, 1932, p. 110.

Meeting at Cambridge

The first member of the Trio to arrive at the university was Goldsworthy Dickinson (Fig. 1). Affectionately known as 'Goldie' to those close to him, he came to King's College as an exhibitioner in 1881.[14] It was there that Dickinson acquired the 'people, music, books and scenery'[15] most important to him. Influenced by his mentor Oscar Browning's 'Socratic gift of maieusis' and 'gripped' by Percy Shelley's 'passionate and ideal love', Dickinson's intellectual curiosities and political interests blossomed.[16] The loss of his mother at the end of his freshman year only cemented his desire to form close relationships with the institution and its members, especially Roger Fry, who enrolled at King's College in 1884 to study natural sciences (Fig. 2). A sensitive character who, whilst capable of careful analysis, tended to act on impulse, Fry found at Cambridge the intellectual home he had long sought. Although their passion was never consummated, the relationship was a 'perfect friendship' that had a 'married feeling', fostering mutual intellectual inspiration.[17] Intimate correspondence in which Dickinson ardently calls out 'Roger, my Roger!', and Fry's affectionate calling of 'my very dear Goldie' extended beyond life at King's.[18] Having followed Dickinson by joining the Apostles,[19]

---

14 C. Froula, 'War, Peace, and Internationalism', in *The Cambridge Companion to the Bloomsbury Group*, ed. V. Rosner, New York 2014, p. 93. An exhibitioner is an individual student at Cambridge who receives a financial award or grant on grounds of merit.

15 E. M. Forster, *Goldsworthy Lowes Dickinson*, London 1962, pp. 26-27.

16 G. Dickinson, in *The Autobiography of G. Lowes Dickinson and Other Unpublished Writings*, ed. D. Proctor, London 1973, pp. 61-65.

17 Ibid., pp. 89-92.

18 G. Dickinson, 'Correspondence between Goldsworthy Lowes Dickinson and REF', The Papers of Roger Eliot Fry, King's College Archive, REF/3/46/1, 14 August 1988; R. Fry, 'Correspondence between Goldsworthy Lowes Dickinson and REF', The Papers of Roger Eliot Fry, King's College Archive, REF/3/46/2, 23 June 1989.

19 Founded in 1820, originally entitled the Cambridge Conversazione Society. See F. Spalding, *Roger Fry: Art and Life*, Berkeley 1980, p. 25. See also W. Lubenow, *The Cambridge Apostles, 1820 – 1914: Liberalism, Imagination, and Friendship in British Intellectual and Professional Life*, Cambridge 1998.

Fig. 1 – Roger Fry, *Goldsworthy Dickinson*, 1925, oil on canvas, 63.8 x 48.5 cm (King's College, Cambridge).

Fig. 2 – Roger Fry, *Self-Portrait*, 1918,
oil on canvas, 79.8 x 59.3 cm
(King's College, Cambridge).

a secret society, Fry was awed and excited by the weekly discussions, and the friendships he formed there became 'so important to him that in after-life [...] he dated everything from them'.[20]

Dickinson's connection with his spiritual home was further strengthened when he secured a Fellowship at King's College in 1887.[21] It was also there that Arthur Waley (Fig. 3), who arrived at the university in 1907, fell under his tutelage.[22] A 'very religious man', Waley's time at King's was cut short as he was forced to withdraw from his classics studies in 1910 due to diminishing eyesight.[23] Heavily influenced by Dickinson, who became a lifelong family friend, in later life Waley missed the intellectual conversations he had held there.[24] He confessed to 'a state of great excitement' at the prospect of seeing Fry, with whom he had become well acquainted, and discussed 'the intellectual topics of the day'.[25] Based on their intellectual curiosity and shared passion for the university, members of the Cambridge Trio continued to rely on each other's guidance and opinions throughout their lives: 'a single soul, like a single labourer, is not sufficient for itself; it dies by isolation'.[26]

---

20 The apostles were founded in 1820, and were originally called the Cambridge Conversazione Society. See F. Spalding, *Roger Fry: Art and Life*, Berkeley 1980, p. 25. See also W. Lubenow, *The Cambridge Apostles, 1820 – 1914: Liberalism, Imagination, and Friendship in British Intellectual and Professional Life*, Cambridge 1998; V. Woolf, *Roger Fry: A Biography*, London 1969, p. 36.

21 Forster, *Goldsworthy Lowes Dickinson* (n. 15), pp. 26-36; 'Dickinson, Goldsworthy Lowes (DKN881GL)', ACAD – A Cambridge Alumni Database, University of Cambridge (website).

22 This drawing was shown in the exhibition *Cambridge Portraits: From Lely to Hockney*, Fitzwilliam Museum, Cambridge 1978, n. 61.

23 C. Goodman, 'Arthur Waley Remembered', *The Charleston Magazine*, 6, 1992 – 1993, p. 8.

24 M. Waley, 'Identifications. Persons to whom copies of poems (1916) were to be given', The Papers of Arthur David Waley, King's College Archive, ADW/1/4, p. 4.

25 A. Waley, 'Intellectual Conversation', *Abinger Chronicle*, 4, 1943, The Papers of Arthur David Waley, King's College Archive, ADW/4/3, p. 34.

26 G. Dickinson, 'The Seekers', The Papers of Goldsworthy Lowes Dickinson, King's College Archive, GLD/6/7A, 1929, pp. 1-8.

Fig. 3 – Michael Ayrton, *Arthur Waley*, 1957, pencil on paper, 31.7 x 34.3 cm (King's College, Cambridge). This drawing was shown in the 1978 exhibition *Cambridge Portraits: From Lely to Hockney*, Fitzwilliam Museum, Cambridge, No. 61.

Finding their Paths

Although he ceased to be a believer in Christianity later in life, Goldsworthy Dickinson remained deeply committed to the idea of social service and devotion.[27] While he briefly studied medicine and attempted a career as a doctor, his devotion to politics superseded all other areas. Lecturing on political science at King's College until his retirement in 1920 and at London School of Economics where he met Xu Zhimo, Dickinson's political ideals were sometimes criticized as 'superior' and 'sheltered', belonging to 'a rich College in the rich University of a rich nation'.[28] Occasionally described as 'eccentric', he was driven by genuine sympathy towards mankind throughout his career.[29] This compassion also partially explains his close friendship with Roger Fry, who, after having unsuccessfully tried to become a painter, transitioned to art history and criticism.[30] Relying on his artistic sensibilities, he soon became a champion of modern art and formalism.[31] As the turn of the twentieth century approached, Dickinson continued to advocate political and social change in his publications such as the 1892 *Revolution and Reaction in Modern France* and the 1896 *The Greek View of Life*. While Dickinson treated Greek politics and culture in a subtly idealized tone, Fry's reputation as a respected art critic was firmly established after his 1899 book on Giovanni Bellini.[32] Although his doctor advised against reading extensively and 'in no case' to pursue a scholarly career, Arthur Waley followed Oswald Sickert's suggestion to consider a position at the British Museum, joining the Department of Oriental Prints and Drawings under

27 R. Fry, 'A Memoir', *Goldsworthy Lowes Dickinson, 6 August 1862, 3 August 1932: Fellow of the College, 1887 – 1932*, Cambridge 1933, p. 5.

28 'Newscuttings and Letter', *The Morning Post*, January 1918, The Papers of Goldsworthy Lowes Dickinson, King's College Archive, GLD/6/4.

29 Harding, 'Goldsworthy Lowes Dickinson' (n. 12), p. 27.

30 A. Bruneau, 'Fry, Roger Eliot', Oxford Dictionary of National Biography (website), 5, 2014.

31 Reed, 'The Fry Collection at the Courtauld Institute Galleries' (n. 11), pp. 766-67.

32 J. Graham, 'A Note on the Early Reputation of Roger Fry', *The Burlington Magazine*, 143 (1181), 2001, p. 495.

the guidance of Laurence Binyon in 1913.[33]

The personal and intellectual paths of the Cambridge Trio continued to intersect. After five years in New York as a curator at the Metropolitan Museum of Art, Roger Fry returned to London in 1910 where some of his friends had begun to gather on Thursday evenings at Thoby Stephen's home, in the then-unfashionable Gordon Square.[34] These weekly gatherings, to which Fry was introduced through Vanessa and Clive Bell, were to become the hub of the Bloomsbury Group that included eclectic individuals, many of whom had previously been members of the Apostles.[35] The Bloomsbury Group has sometimes been described as elitist, snobbish and self-protective, characteristics inconsistent with Fry's personality.[36] A central figure of the group, Fry was not spared criticism, standing accused of having 'poisoned the good name of modernism for the entire century'.[37] Substantial class anxiety is embedded in this condemnation, and yet much is based on misunderstanding, as the 'transcendental emotional experience' before works of art was the central element of the group's sense of modernism.[38] Though not a member, Goldsworthy Dickinson was closely associated with and sympathetic to the Bloomsbury Group, as was Arthur Waley who, after moving to a flat in Gordon Square, spent over forty

---

33 M. Waley, 'Manuscript Memoir of Arthur Waley', The Papers of Arthur David Waley, King's College Archive, ADW/1/1, p. 6; 'He Never Went to China – A Portrait of Arthur Waley' (n. 9), p. 139.

34 V. Rosner, 'Introduction', in *The Cambridge Companion to the Bloomsbury Group*, ed. V. Rosner, New York 2014, p. 3.

35 L. Marcus, 'Bloomsbury Aesthetics', in *The Cambridge Companion to the Bloomsbury Group*, ed. V. Rosner, New York 2014, p. 162.

36 For criticisms of the Bloomsbury Group, see C. Harrison, *English Art and Modernism, 1900 – 39*, New Haven 1981, pp. 32, 57, 88, 90; for Fry, see C. Green, 'Into the Twentieth Century: Roger Fry's Project Seen from 2000', in *Art Made Modern: Roger Fry's Vision of Art*, ed. C. Green, London 2000, pp. 13-14.

37 C. Reed, 'Roger Fry: The Art of Bloomsbury. San Marino and London', *The Burlington Magazine*, 142 (1165), 2000, p. 263.

38 Ibid., p. 264; C. Reed, *A Roger Fry Reader*, Chicago and London 1996, p. 58.

years living in the area and interacted with many of the group's members.[39] Closely acquainted with the Bloomsbury Group, Xu Zhimo drew inspiration from its artists and writers to initiate a sister movement in China.

---

39 'He Never Went to China – A Portrait of Arthur Waley' (n. 9), p. 140.

The Three Chinamen

Goldsworthy Dickinson's foray into Chinese art was driven by his view that the country could serve as inspiration for the salvation of the modern Western world. Inspired by the pioneering translations of Chinese classics by Herbert Giles, as well as by Eugène Simon's depiction of a peaceful agrarian nation in the 1885 *La cité chinoise*, Dickinson wrote *Letters from John Chinaman.*[40] Meant to provide an outsider's view of the 'malaise' of the West, the suggestion to have the foreign critic be Chinese came from Roger Fry.[41] Published in 1901, the same year that Fry published his first article on Chinese art, and during a period of high 'jingoistic' British hostility towards China, Dickinson resorted to anonymous letters in which a fictive Chinese official accused the West of commercialism and imperialism.[42] So vivid were his accounts that the work was sometimes mistaken for that of a native Chinese author. The American politician William Bryan went so far as to state that the author had never seen 'the inside of a Christian home'.[43] Fry, in the meantime, praised the 'high standard of craftsmanship', the sensitivity to material and the 'strenuous desire for perfection' of Chinese art, seeking 'to dispel the popular theory that Chinese civilisation is not only different, but also inferior to our own'.[44] This notion was reasserted in his subsequent publications on the topic, which numbered over twenty, and evidenced by his posthumously published *Last*

---

40 Harding, 'Goldsworthy Lowes Dickinson' (n. 12), p. 29.

41 P. Hardie, 'Ferdinand Schiller, Collecting Chinese Art 1913 – 1936', *Journal of Museum Ethnography*, 15, 2003, pp. 35-46.

42 R. Fry, 'Chinese Art at the Whitechapel Gallery' (n. 6), p. 165; Harding, 'Goldsworthy Lowes Dickinson' (n. 12), p. 29.

43 E. M. Forster, 'Introduction', *Letters from John Chinaman and Other Essays*, London 1946, pp. 7-10 (9). There is a tradition of epistolary novel in European literature as early as the fifteenth century, in which documents such as letters are used to mimic real life situations, adding realism to the narrative. Meant to reflect an external view, the narrator is often said to be a foreigner.

44 Fry, 'Chinese Art at the Whitechapel Gallery' (n. 7), p. 165.

Lectures.[45] It was this shared interest in Chinese art that solidified Fry's lifelong friendship with Dickinson.[46]

By the time Roger Fry was appointed Slade Professor of Fine Art at the University of Cambridge, he had challenged the status quo by transforming the perception of art for generations to come. Despite limited resources, repeated financial crises, and a generosity that constrained his spending, Fry accumulated artworks throughout his lifetime, including a small sample of Chinese objects.[47] Exhibited in conjunction with Samuel Courtauld's art collection at Home House, London, more than one hundred objects were displayed, including six Chinese bronze plaques and eight Chinese ceramics, such as the Qing (1644 – 1911) vase (Fig. 4) shown in his self-portrait (Fig. 2).[48] The collection offers a precious art-historical record of the development of modernist aesthetics, as well as a prism into Fry's formalism, and presents a vivid expression of the 'Bloomsbury taste'.[49] This appreciation of Chinese art was shared by his protégé, Arthur Waley. Having read Laurence Binyon's *Painting in the Far East*, which depicted dialogue between Chinese and Greek artistic traditions, Waley further developed his appreciation of Chinese paintings at the British Museum.[50] He compiled an

45 Fry considered devoting a whole term in 1934 to Chinese art. See R. Fry, *Letters of Roger Fry*, ed. D. Sutton, vol. II, London 1972, p. 690.

46 S. Fishman, 'Roger Fry', *The Interpretation of Art*, Berkeley and Los Angeles 1963, p. 101.

47 Reed, 'The Fry Collection at the Courtauld Institute Galleries' (n. 11), pp. 766-67.

48 See The Home House Trustees, *Catalogue of the Pictures and other Works of Art at Home House*, London 1935, pp. 59-84.

49 Reed, 'The Fry Collection at the Courtauld Institute Galleries' (n. 11), p. 766; Courtauld Institute of Art, *Catalogue of the Fry Collection*, London 1958, p. 3.

50 L. Binyon, *Painting in the Far East: An Introduction to the History of Pictorial Art in Asia Especially China and Japan*, London 1913, pp. 1-38 (29). The British Museum's Chinese paintings were mainly comprised of the bequest of William Anderson, who had paid special attention to Song and Ming dynasties, as well as the collection of Olga-Julia Wegener who had a preference for birds, flowers and figures. See M. Huang, 'British Interest in Chinese Painting, 1881 – 1910', *Journal of the History of Collections*, 22, 2010, pp. 279-87. For the British Museum early catalogues of Chinese art, see A. Stein, *Guide to an Exhibition of Paintings, Manuscripts, and Other Archaeological Objects Collected by Sir Aurel Stein in Chinese Turkestan*, London 1914; R. Hobson, *Chinese Art. One Hundred Plates in Colour. Introduced by an Outline Sketch of Chinese Art*, London 1927.

Fig. 4 – *Vase with Rudimentary Elephant-Head Handles*, 18th century, ceramic, H. 31.5 cm, W. 21.5 cm (The Courtauld Gallery, London).

index of Chinese and Japanese painters while cataloguing the museum's Dunhuang paintings recovered by Marc Aurel Stein, a project for which Waley taught himself Chinese and Japanese.[51] Binyon, who claimed that in China painting was a passion rather than a profession, was supportive of his linguistic studies, allowing him to pursue them with little interruption.[52]

Arthur Waley's translation of fifty-two Chinese poems, privately printed in 1916 at Roger Fry's persuasion, was first distributed among close friends.[53] The complete volume, *A Hundred and Seventy Chinese Poems*, was compiled two years later.[54] Unlike Herbert Giles's 1901 *A History of Chinese Literature*, which drew parallels between Chinese and ancient Greek literature and claimed to be 'the first of its kind',[55] Waley recreated Chinese poetry in a mode closer to the contemporary English prose of T. S. Eliot and Ezra Pound.[56] Determined that his books should not merely be addressed to fellow scholars, his study contributed to the appropriation of Chinese poetry by the West.[57] As Fry wrote of Waley's translations of Han (206 BC – AD 220) poems, 'they have such simplicity and absence of rhetoric that they are quite in keeping with today's taste'.[58] Although debate on the subtle differences between Waley's renderings and those of his contemporaries exists and his translations of Chinese literature

---

51 Arthur Waley's 1922 *An Index of Chinese Artists Represented in the Sub-Department of Oriental Prints and Drawings in the British Museum* was the first compilation of Chinese artists in the West. See B. Gray, 'Waley, Arthur David', rev. G. Dudbridge, Oxford Dictionary of National Biography (website).

52 L. Binyon, 'Chinese Painting', in *China Body & Soul*, ed. E. Hughes, London 1938, p. 20; Waley, 'Identifications. Persons to whom copies of poems (1916) were to be given' (n. 24).

53 'He Never Went to China – A Portrait of Arthur Waley' (n. 9), p. 140.

54 Gray, 'Waley, Arthur David' (n. 51).

55 Harding, 'Goldsworthy Lowes Dickinson' (n. 12), p. 34.

56 M. Nylan, 'Arthur Waley and Li Zehou: Two Aesthetes Translating', *Art in Translation*, 5, 2013, p. 167.

57 D. Waley, 'Arthur Waley: A Memoir', 2001, The Papers of Arthur David Waley, King's College Archive, ADW/1/6.

58 Fry, *Letters of Roger Fry* (n. 45), vol. II, p. 408.

and philosophy were widely circulated, his writings on Chinese art received less attention.[59] One of Waley's first articles on the subject, 'A Chinese Picture' was published in 1917 in *The Burlington Magazine for Connoisseurs*, a periodical co-founded by Fry in 1903.[60] An important series of nine essays entitled 'Chinese Philosophy of Art' appeared in the same magazine in the early 1920s, examining Chinese art theorists from Xie He of the fifth century to Dong Qichang of the Ming dynasty (1368 – 1644). As neither a 'reasoned sequence of thoughts' nor 'systematic art-philosophy' by Chinese writers had been developed, Waley had to rely on 'casual observations, conversations, anecdotes and opinions' to construct his own Chinese art history.[61] *An Introduction to the Study of Chinese Painting*, 'a by-product' of his unpublished notes, is Waley's most systematic presentation on the subject.[62] Like Fry, who championed the modernity of Chinese art, Waley believed that 'a rough parity' existed between the classical East and West, and that parallels between traditional Chinese and contemporary European art abounded.[63]

---

59 See C. Tomlinson, 'Introduction', *The Oxford Book of Verse in English Translation*, Oxford 1980, p. VIII; W. Yeats, 'Introduction', *The Oxford Book of Modern Verse*, Oxford 1936, p. XI.

60 F. Johns, *A Bibliography of Arthur Waley*, London 1968, p. 111.

61 A. Waley, 'Chinese Philosophy of Art – IX. (Concluded)', *The Burlington Magazine for Connoisseurs*, 39 (225), 1921, p. 297.

62 Gray, 'Waley, Arthur David' (n. 51).

63 Nylan, 'Arthur Waley and Li Zehou: Two Aesthetes Translating' (n. 56), p. 166.

The Discovery of Chinese Art in the West

At the dawn of the twentieth century, England's academic elite increasingly looked beyond its own borders for cultural histories to explore. The historical superiority of Chinese civilisation, which lasted until the ascendancy of the Western World during the Ming dynasty,[64] made China into a magnet of curiosity for numerous intellectuals. While railway construction saw collaboration with foreign technicians, events such as the Boxer Rebellion and Opium Wars led to a substantial outflow of art.[65] The important Chinese art trade began in the late nineteenth century, and soon resulted in an increased presence of Chinese art in European collections. The George Eumorfopoulos as well as the Adolphe Stoclet collections, coupled with objects brought back from Paul Pelliot's and Marc Aurel Stein's expeditions, gave scholars, including the Cambridge Trio, an opportunity to examine Chinese art up close. Passions for fresh visual sensations were strong, offering wide possibilities for pure aesthetic criticism when contextual knowledge was lacking.[66]

Despite the presence of serious collectors such as John Gray and Robert Davidson, as well as the rococo inspired chinoiserie frenzy more than a century earlier, Chinese art was still perceived as decorative and inferior to its Western counterparts.[67] In Germany, the establishment of an Islamic art department in 1904 and an Oriental art department in 1906 in the original Royal Museum (Koenigliches Museum) in Berlin, followed by the founding of the Museum of East Asian Art in Cologne, led to the inception of 'world art history' in German speaking countries. Although art history was established as a discipline in the second

64 The British Museum, *Ming: 50 Years that Changed China*, London 2014, pp. 25, 256-92.

65 'George Aristedes Eumorfopoulos 1863 – 1939 Collector, Businessman, and Philanthropist', *The Smithsonian's Museums of Asian Art*, 29 February 2016.

66 L. Einstein, 'Some Notes on Chinese Painting', *The Burlington Magazine for Connoisseurs*, 21 (112), 1912, p. 185.

67 *Collectors: Individuals and Institutions*, ed. A. Shelton, London 2001, pp. 111-61.

68 L. Ledderose, 'Kunstgeschichte und Weltkunstgeschichte', *Saeculun*, 40 (2), 1989, p. 136.

half of the nineteenth century in Germanic regions, East Asian art history departments were not established until 1912, when Josef Strzygowski of the University of Vienna became Chair of the Art of the Near East, a prelude to decades of effort to establish East Asian art as an academic discipline based on the methods and standards formulated for European art history in German countries.[69] Otto Kümmel's 1921 *Die Kunst Ostasiens* and his 1929 the *Ausstellung chinesischer Kunst*, as well as Otto Fischer's 1921 *Chinesische Landschaftsmalerei* and his 1928 *Die Kunst Indiens, Chinas und Japans*, amongst others, were successful in this endeavour. Nevertheless, German scholarship was sometimes criticized for achieving nothing further than a 'piling up of facts'. Raphael Petrucci wrote to his close friend Laurence Binyon in 1908 that the recently published book on Chinese art by Oskar Münsterberg was 'made up of bits and pieces, pillaged from all the world', a feature 'characteristic of Germany'.[70] In England too, serious academic study had not yet been established, and it would not be until the early twentieth century that Chinese objects came to be defined as 'Chinese art' as opposed to 'Oriental object[s]'.[71] The founding of the Oriental Ceramic Society in 1921 marked serious scholarly interest in the subject, while collections such as that of Percival David, amassed between WWI and WWII, offered further visual stimulation as well as study material.[72]

While Roger Fry was supposedly introduced to Chinese art in America by Matthew Prichard of the Boston Museum of Fine Arts in 1905, Goldsworthy Dickinson's interest was spawned by

---

69 Ibid.

70 B. Gray, 'The Development of Taste in Chinese Art in the West 1872 – 1972', *Studies in Chinese and Islamic Art, vol. I Chinese Art*, London 1985, pp. 19-20. *Originally published in Transactions of the Oriental Ceramic Society*, 39, 1971 – 1973, p. 18.

71 S. Pierson, 'From Market and Exhibition to University: Sir Percival David and the Institutionalization of Chinese Art History in England', in *Collecting China: The World, China, and a History of Collecting*, ed. V. Rujivacharakul, Plymouth 2011, p. 131.

72 Presented to the University of London in 1950 by Sir Percival David, the collection is now on permanent display at the British Museum.

his inquiries into Chinese society.[73] Given the lack of Asian art material and scholarship in England, most information was gathered from continental Europe, especially France.[74] The study of Chinese art was stimulated by the opening of the Musée Guimet and Musée Cernuschi in Paris in the late nineteenth century, although it was soon overtaken by the United States, where Ernest Fenollosa played a vital role.[75] While Fenollosa's appointment to the Boston Museum of Fine Arts in 1890 did not last long and his influential book, *The Epochs of Chinese and Japanese Art*, was only published posthumously in 1912, his views, including the idea that the Far East had attained to a culture comparable to the peak of Greece and the Renaissance, were widely disseminated in the United States by lectures given between 1895 and 1908.[76] Fenollosa was not alone in analysing Chinese art through traditional Japanese scholarship, as Sir Purdon Clark of the Metropolitan Museum of Art declared in 1906 that it would be 'nonsense' to distinguish Chinese from Japanese art, an opinion that Fry considered exemplary of 'mid-Victorian taste'.[77] Whilst Charles Freer's burgeoning collection of Oriental art was initially assisted by Fenollosa's consultancy, Freer recognized 'deeper' and 'wider' interest in the topic by the end of the first decade of the twentieth century, by which time Fry had returned to Europe.[78] Although exposed to numerous objects and theories while employed at the Metropolitan Museum of Art, it was in his repeated visits to France that Fry would 'find his greatest inspiration as a critic'.[79] His exposure to amateurs and dealers in Paris who avidly collected Chinese art broadened his taste. As he confessed to his old Cambridge friend Dickinson, 'the East is thoroughly ransacked by art dealers' and 'one can learn more

73 L. Sorensen, 'Fry, Roger', Dictionary of Art Historians (website).

74 R. Fry, 'Review of *The Year-Book of Oriental Art and Culture 1924 – 1925*. Edited by Arthur Waley', Nation and Athenaeum, 1925, p. 650.

75 Gray, 'The Development of Taste in Chinese Art in the West 1872 – 1972' (n. 70), pp. 17-23.

76 Ibid., p. 18.

77 Fry, *Letters of Roger Fry* (n. 45), vol. I, p. 273.

78 Gray, 'The Development of Taste in Chinese Art in the West 1872 – 1972' (n. 70), p. 18.

79 Woolf, *Roger Fry: A Biography* (n. 20), p. 81.

about the best things in Paris than in Pekin'.[80]

Prompted by Ezra Pound's *second-hand* translation of Chinese literature from French, Arthur Waley decided to do the same from the original source.[81] Approaching Chinese art from a literary perspective, he may have also been inspired by Raphael Petrucci, who approached the history of Chinese art with the aid of philosophy and theology.[82] Early French scholarship, led by Edouard Chavannes whose *La Sculpture sur pierre en Chine au temps des deux dynasties Han* appeared as early as in 1893, was best represented by Petrucci, whose 1910 *La philosophie de la nature dans l'art d'Extrême-Orient* not only treated Chinese art from a wider aesthetic perspective, but also assumed painting to be the overarching art form.[83] This opinion was shared by and extended upon by René Grousset, curator of Musée Cernuschi and Musée Guimet in Paris. Grousset published his four volume *Les civilisations de l'Orient* in 1929 and 1930, in which a purely archaeological view was taken for the first time. In his 1936 *L'art de l'Extrême Orient: paysages, fleurs, animaux*, he argued that Chinese paintings were the exact opposite of anthropomorphism and that human beings tended to disappear before the mysterious and omnipresent Nature, a view reminiscent of that of the Cambridge Trio.[84] Goldsworthy Dickinson, who claimed to have been a Chinaman 'in a previous existence',[85] meanwhile appropriated the praise of 'humanity' as 'a fraternal association of equal individuals' of Republican idealism, transposing the theory of democracy of modern France onto his idealized vision of China.[86] Relying on the work of his fellow Cambridge Trio members, Roger Fry

80 Fry, *Letters of Roger Fry* (n. 45), vol. II, p. 368.

81 Laurence, *Lily Briscoe's Chinese Eyes: Bloomsbury, Modernism, and China* (n. 10), p. 309.

82 R. Fry. 'Review of *La philosophie de la nature dans l'art d'Extrême-Orient* by Raphael Petrucci', *The Burlington Magazine for Connoisseurs*, 19, 1911, pp. 106-7.

83 Gray, 'The Development of Taste in Chinese Art in the West 1872 – 1972' (n. 70), p. 19.

84 R. Grousset, *L'art de l'Extrême Orient: paysages, fleurs, animaux*, Paris 1936, p. 5.

85 Forster, *Goldsworthy Lowes Dickinson* (n. 15), p. 142.

86 G. Dickinson, 'The People as Humanity', *Revolution and Reaction in Modern France*, London 1892, pp. 128-32.

would lay the foundation for some of his groundbreaking research on Chinese art that would challenge the Western canon.

THE DISCUSSION OF THE MODERNITY OF CHINESE ART

Aesthetics, Connoisseurship and Society

Roger Fry: Formalism and Aesthetics

The Western approach to Chinese art has been typified by Basil Gray as an original 'curiosity-hunger' antiquarianism during the eighteenth century, which developed into a 'knowledge-hunger' driven by the sudden availability of Chinese goods, until an 'aesthetic' approach was finally adopted, a movement in which 'Roger Fry was a key figure, who sought for a unity in all great periods of art.'[87] Fry confessed that his work had always had 'some kind of aesthetic', had been 'a purely practical' tentative means to bring his 'aesthetic impressions' into order.[88] Fry's conjecture about Chinese art stems from his visual approach, an ever-evolving process best explained in his 1909 'An Essay in Aesthetics' in which relations between art and life, emotion and nature, are explored. For him, a work of art is 'intimately connected' with the 'imaginary life' where we can abstract ourselves from our 'actual life' and where immediate 'responsive reaction' is not necessary. Rather than a 'copy of actual life', a work of art allows free and sincere expression of the imagination. This freedom from external conditions permits our imaginative life to perceive and recognise objects beyond 'needful' purposes; eliciting a 'greater purity and freedom' of emotion in that we can 'feel' and 'watch' from a distance.[89] This concept is further elaborated in Fry's subsequent essay 'Some Questions in Esthetics' in 1926, in which the 'esthetic emotion' is not about sensations, objects, persons or events, but rather an 'attentive passivity' to the effects of sensations achieved through a 'special orientation of the consciousness' and a 'focusing of the attention'.[90] This is an 'applied aesthetics' that artists could rely upon when producing work.[91]

87 Gray, 'The Development of Taste in Chinese Art in the West 1872 – 1972' (n. 70), pp. 19-41.

88 R. Fry, 'Retrospect', *Vision and Design*, London 1981, p. 199.

89 Fry, 'An Essay in Aesthetics' (n. 11), pp. 16-38.

90 R. Fry, 'Some Questions in Esthetics', *Transformations*, New York 1968, p. 5.

91 R. Fry, 'Introduction', in J. Reynolds, *Discourses*, London 1905, p. x.

Roger Fry's asserted debt to Lev Nikolayevich Tolstoy, who defined the function of art as the expression of emotion, may have inspired his emotional aesthetic engagement.[92] For Tolstoy, the concept of art was a basic human condition capable of 'intercourse' between men, with its activity based on 'a man receiving' 'another man's expression of feeling'.[93] Fry considered Tolstoy's 1898 *What is Art?* as marking the 'beginning of fruitful speculation in aesthetic', suggesting that art had no special concern with beauty in nature but is '*par excellence* the language of emotion'.[94] This emotion is never identical with feeling in actual life, but rather a detached apprehension that leads to the direct outcome of form, the 'most essential quality' of an artwork. Responses to works of art should also be distinct from those resulting from other life situations.[95] Contemplating form, the viewer is able to 'travel in an opposite direction' to arrive at the original emotion.[96] It has been suggested that Fry's relationship with Bernard Berenson contributed to the formation of his emotional engagement with art in combination with connoisseurship's empirical exploration.[97] Emphasizing visual language in art appreciation, Berenson's priority was to arouse self-awareness and reactions during visual experiences.[98] For Fry, art should appreciate emotion 'in and for itself'.[99] This concept was not new but rather the result of Fry's lengthy evolution, from classic to modern. He contended that art should serve as 'a mode of expression of human experience' achieved through 'chiaroscuro and colour'.[100] The proper 'aesthetic attitude' should be characterized by 'clear disinterested contemplation' arrived at

---

92 Reed, *A Roger Fry Reader* (n. 38), pp. 11 and 154.

93 L. Tolstoy, *What is Art?*, transl. A. Maude, 1899, Chapter V.

94 Fry, 'Retrospect' (n. 88), pp. 204-5.

95 Fry, 'Some Questions in Esthetics' (n. 90), p. 2.

96 Fry, 'Retrospect' (n. 88), pp. 204-5.

97 Green, 'Into the Twentieth Century: Roger Fry's Project Seen from 2000' (n. 36), p. 18.

98 B. Berenson, *The Italian Painters of the Renaissance*, Oxford 1980, pp. ix-xiii.

99 Fry, 'An Essay in Aesthetics' (n. 11), pp. 30-35.

100 Fry, 'Introduction' (n. 91), pp. ix-xix.

via 'order' and 'variety'; the resultant 'aesthetic approval' is called 'beauty'. Nature as well as 'natural forms' are appropriated only for the conscious purpose of arousing 'aesthetic feeling', regardless of representation or abstraction.[101]

Roger Fry interpreted world art with an emphasis on form over content and context, relying upon its formal qualities assessed by his aesthetic approach. Judging pictures by contemporary standards, many critics condemned the lack of perspective in Chinese painting while Fry praised its modernist vision.[102] For Fry, a Chinese painting, whether hanging or handscroll, was beautiful if it displayed unity in its pictorial design, a chief aspect of 'order'. The length of a scroll often requires looking at the picture in 'successive segments' as the viewer unrolls and rolls it at each end; a 'successive unity' would be achieved were each element in 'harmonious relation' with the preceding part.[103] For Fry, the eleventh-century painting attributed to Northern Song (960 – 1127) painter Li Longmian (Fig. 5) relies on uncomplicated linear design to convey emotion.[104] The space and atmosphere of the woodland scene is transmitted through 'simple economic lines' whose 'strange evocative power' effectively conveys a remote and mysterious mood, creating empathetic emotions with the artist and the hermit figure in 'profound meditation' through shapes and tone washes.[105] Li was renowned for appropriating the *bai miao* (drawing in fine ink line) style into *wen ren hua* (literati painting), while his practice of collecting and imitating antique paintings led to the classic style of his lines.[106] Unaware of this

101 Fry, 'An Essay in Aesthetics' (n. 11), pp. 36-8.

102 J. Burling and A. Burling, *Chinese Art*, New York 1953, p. 40.

103 Fry, 'An Essay in Aesthetics' (n. 11), pp. 31-33.

104 Image from Royal Academy of Arts, *A Commemorative Catalogue of the International Exhibition of Chinese Art*, London 1936, Lot 1036 (lent by Adolphe Stoclet, Brussels). Illustrated in R. Fry, *Last Lectures*, Cambridge 1939, pl. 245.

105 Fry, *Last Lectures* (n. 104), p. 148.

106 G. Suzuki, 'Li Gonglin', *Zhong Guo Hui Hua Shi (Chinese Painting History)*, vol. I, transl. M. Wei, Taipei 1987, pp. 246-59.

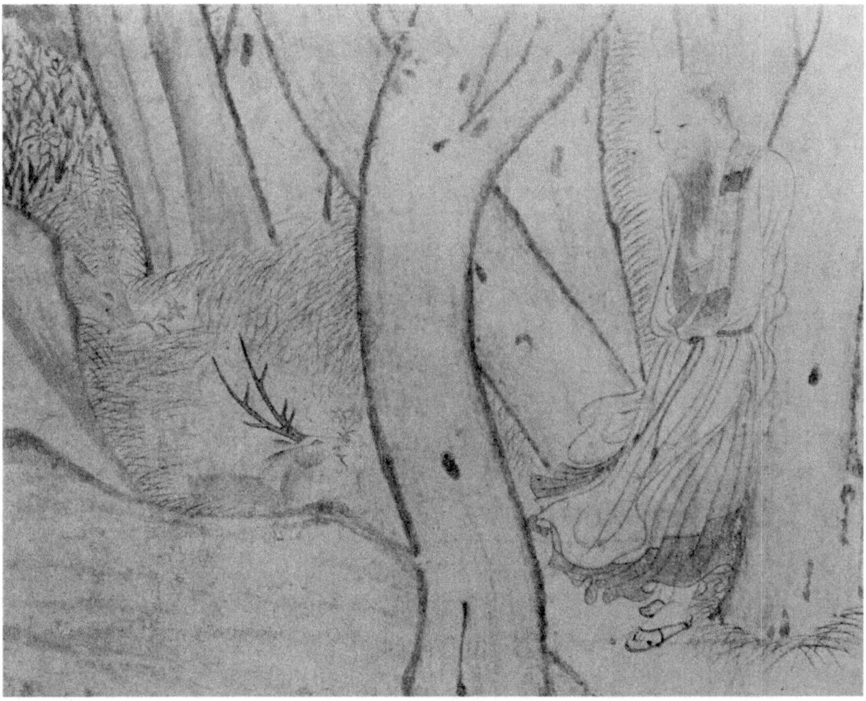

Fig. 5 – A follower of Li Longmian, *A Sage in the Forest*, possibly Yuan dynasty (1271 – 1368), ink on paper, 26.0 x 32.0 cm, image from Royal Academy of Arts, *A Commemorative Catalogue of the International Exhibition of Chinese Art*, London, 1936, Lot 1036 (lent by Adolphe Stoclet, Brussels). Illustrated in R. Fry, *Last Lectures*, Cambridge, 1939, Pl. 245.

background, Fry was able to deduce similar conclusions through visual features. Imbuing emotional responses in formal aspects of a painting via which similar feelings in the viewer could be aroused was already present in Zong Bin's fifth-century 'Hua Shan Shui Xu' ('Preface to Landscape Paintings'), where he stated that 'a truth perceived by someone long, long ago can be understood by those coming a thousand years after'.[107] Despite the notion that Chinese paintings lacked perspective, the artist reflected more actively on 'perspective in the relation of his figures' than his early European counterparts, as the former had a 'mature instinctive feeling for the relation of these figures' not fixed in 'rigid principle'.[108] Fry's approach allows an otherwise-unintelligible Chinese picture to arouse strong aesthetic experiences in Western viewers ignorant of its culture and context.

Roger Fry's formalist approach included the dating of Chinese art. Aesthetic pleasures could be derived from intimate connections with 'the creative spirit of the artist', which he associated with the 'general mentality' of the period represented in artistic forms. Juxtaposing two *You* bronzes of the Zhou (1046 – 256 BC) period, he wrote that one of them (Fig. 6), with its outstanding flanges and ridged projections, gave 'to the pot a suggestion of terrific force, an almost menacing quality'.[109] The other *You* (Fig. 7) was nearly the complete antithesis, a perfect example showing 'the classic quality of Chinese art' in 'its clear and articulate statement of the main relations'.[110] Discussing the chronological order of the *Yous*, he argued that the 'classic' bronze was the product of a progressive sophisticated and refined culture and thus later, while the 'barbaric aggressiveness' of its counterpart was a sign of an earlier, less civilised society.[111]

---

107 *The Chinese Theory of Art*, transl. Y. Lin, London 1967, pp. 31-33.

108 R. Fry, 'Drawing or Design', The Papers of Roger Eliot Fry, King's College Archive, REF/1/131, 1920 – 1929.

109 Illustrated in Fry, *Last Lectures* (n. 104), pl. 143.

110 Illustrated in Fry, *Last Lectures* (n. 104), pl. 144, as *Late Yu*.

111 Fry, *Last Lectures* (n. 104), pp. 108-10.

Fig. 6 – *You from Altar Stand*, Western Zhou dynasty (1046 – 771 BC), bronze (The Metropolitan Museum of Art, New York). Illustrated in R. Fry, *Last Lectures*, Cambridge, 1939, Pl. 143.

Fig. 7 – *Wine Jar You*, late Shang dynast (1600 – 1046 BC), bronze, H. 34.2 cm, W. 29.7 cm (Victoria and Albert Museum, London, formerly Eumorfopoulos collection). Illustrated in R. Fry, *Last Lectures*, Cambridge, 1939, Pl. 144, as *Late Yu*.

For Fry, the first item was 'essentially primitive' as the artist was intent on bestowing his imagery with 'utmost expressive force' in a 'passionate determination struggling with difficulty', whereas the second was the work of a conscious artist and belonged to a group of highly developed art. Given that Zhou culture transitioned from early brutality towards Confucian beauty and delicacy, Fry mistakenly concluded that the second object must be more recent due to its higher culture. As archaeological discoveries would subsequently confirm, the first *You*, however, was Western Zhou (1046 – 771 BC),[112] whereas the second late Shang (1600 – 1046 BC) and therefore earlier.[113] Fry's dating inaccuracy needs to be interpreted in the context of the infancy of archaeology in China, where accidental discoveries were coupled with extensive raids of Shang tombs and limited dating beyond the Zhou dynasty. Relying on scarce Shang material and few reference objects accessible only through reproductions, Fry failed to notice subtle differences in representational strategies.[114] This being said, Zhou bronzes have been considered inferior and derivatives of their Shang predecessors by both academics and collectors, making Fry's pioneering insight, that the 'classic' example is of a higher culture, impressive.[115]

Arthur Waley: Knowledge and Connoisseurship

For Arthur Waley, connoisseurship consisted not in aesthetics but rather in 'the ability to decide who brought it into being', which is subject to 'knowledge' of science rather than 'sensitivity' of inspiration. Here acquaintance with Chinese civilization, tradition and history is vital for the appreciation of its art, for 'some degree of intellectual curiosity' naturally accompanies a

---

112 See comparative object from tomb of the Marquis of Haihun of Western Han (206 BC – AD 24) in Nanchang, Jiangxi, excavated between 2011 and 2016.

113 Victoria and Albert Museum, London, no. M.6:1,2-1935, Wine jar, 1200 – 1050 BC.

114 See examples in *The Collection of Old Bronzes of Sumitomo*, ed. S. Umehara, Kyoto 1971, pl. 47 and 53.

115 R. Thorp, *China in the Early Bronze Age: Shang Civilization*, Philadelphia 2005, pp. 244-49; W. Hung, *Monumentality in Early Chinese Art and Architecture*, Stanford 1995, pp. 53-63.

human being's 'sensitivity to art'. Waley believed that the enjoyment of art inevitably led to questions about the makers and their world, inquiries which could best be addressed through the thorough examination of literature, 'principally' poetry.[116] For Waley, visual evidence constituted knowledge. This line of reasoning is evidenced by his catalogue of Dunhuang paintings, which includes a discussion of the possibilities of pigment analysis could assist with dating.[117] A conscientious classics scholar, Waley acquired the majority of his expertise from primary Chinese sources, covering literature from *Li Dai Ming Hua Ji (Famous Paintings Through History)*, the ancestor of Chinese painting history, to the Qing imperial collection catalogue *Shi Qü Bao Ji (Precious Book Box of the Stone Drain)*.[118] Relying on his linguistic prowess, Waley aimed to convey the backgrounds and feelings of Chinese artists which he deemed crucial to the Occidental reader. He subtly corrected inaccuracies of other Western scholars, stressing for instance that Raphael Petrucci's translation of Xie He's second principle as 'la loi des os au moyen du pinceau' was meaningless as *fa* had been wrongly translated into *loi*, or that the 'immobilité d'esprit' he found so 'felicitous' never occurred in the original Chinese text.[119]

Arthur Waley's knowledge-based connoisseurship allowed him to explore otherwise inaccessible research avenues. Praised as a 'Renaissance man', his profound sensibility and aesthetic empathy led him to distinguished scholarly achievements.[120]

116 A. Waley, *An Introduction to the Study of Chinese Painting*, London 1958 (First published 1923), pp. 3-4.

117 For detail see A. Waley, *A Catalogue of Paintings Recovered from Tun-Huang by Sir Aurel Stein, K. C. I. E.*, London 1931, p. ix.

118 *Li Dai Ming Hua Ji*, by Zhang Yanyuan, completed in 847; for a discussion, see Y. Zhang, *Li Dai Ming Hua Ji*, ed. J. Yü, Shanghai 1964, pp. 211-12; *Shi Qü Bao Ji*, catalogue of the secular pictures in the Emperor Qianlong collection, first published in Shanghai, 1918. For reference detail see Waley, *An Introduction* (n. 116), pp. 253-54.

119 *Li Dai Ming Hua Ji*, by Zhang Yanyuan, completed in 847; Y. Zhang, *Li Dai Ming Hua Ji*, ed. J. Yü, Shanghai 1964, pp. 211-12; A. Waley, 'Chinese Philosophy of Art – IV. Kuo His (Part I)', *The Burlington Magazine for Connoisseurs*, 38 (218), 1921, p. 247.

120 Morris, 'Arthur Waley' (n. 9), pp. 52-53.

Examining the painting *Qing Ming Shang He Tu (Going up the River for the Spring Festival)* (Figs. 8 and 9), he stressed the artist's 'realistic representation' of the scene as dictated by Emperor Huizong.[121] It was this 'pictorial record' of the Bian River that explained why this painting was distinct from traditional Northern Song style, an observation referenced by subsequent scholars such as William Cohn.[122] Historical accounts of the sack of Bian City (present day Kaifeng) by the Jin Tartars shortly after the painting was completed explain why Chinese accounts of it were full of 'sentiment of *then* and *now*'.[123] Uninhibited by the lack of Chinese literature, Waley translated the painting's inscriptions, demonstrating its provenance and the fate it suffered. This contextual information not only allowed Western audiences to appreciate the realist style as a departure from contemporary tradition, but also furthered an understanding of the emotion and sentiment at play. Observing these elements was more advanced and refined than the analysis of some later art historians such as Laurence Sickman who, when referring to the painting's original version at the Palace Museum, only superficially described the documentary nature and technical skill of the scroll.[124] As Waley stated in 'The Rarity of Ancient Chinese Paintings', the study of Chinese painting is hindered by the unknown fate of many originals and the existence of numerous copies without definite attribution. Waley also learned of Chinese painting from publications and reproductions, such as the Japanese Magazine *Kokka*. Using Tang (618 – 907) works as an example, he agreed with Dong Qichang on the importance of seeing the original and taking as standard 'things we have actually seen'.[125] In contrast to

---

121 Illustrated in A. Waley, 'A Chinese Picture', The Burlington Magazine for Connoisseurs, 30 (166), 1917, pl. I-II.

122 A. Waley, 'A Chinese Picture', *The Burlington Magazine for Connoisseurs*, 30 (166), 1917, p. 3. This observation is referred to by later scholars; see, for instance, W. Cohn, *Chinese Painting*, London 1948, p. 75.

123 Waley, 'A Chinese Picture' (n. 121), p. 4.

124 L. Sickman and A. Soper, *The Art and Architecture of China*, Baltimore 1968, pp. 119-20.

125 A. Waley, 'The Rarity of Ancient Chinese Paintings', *The Burlington Magazine for Connoisseurs*, 30 (171), 1917, p. 209.

Fig. 8 – After Zhang Zeduan, the bridge section of *Going up the River for the Spring Festival*, Southern Song dynasty (1127 – 1279), handscroll, ink and colour on silk, 29.2 x 624.8 cm (The British Museum, London). Illustrated in A. Waley, 'A Chinese Picture', *The Burlington Magazine for Connoisseurs*, 30 (166), 1917, Pl. I.

Fig. 9 – After Zhang Zeduan, the wall section of *Going up the River for the Spring Festival,* Southern Song dynasty (1127 – 1279), handscroll, ink and colour on silk, 29.2 x 624.8 cm (The British Museum, London). Illustrated in A. Waley, 'A Chinese Picture', *The Burlington Magazine for Connoisseurs*, 30 (166), 1917, Pl. II.

Roger Fry, who ventured into formal analysis while acknowledging that copies of masterpieces in China were treasured with 'almost equal veneration', complicating the establishment of a fixed point of reference, Waley was more cautious, choosing to present the facts.[126]

Arthur Waley was the first to label the painting in Adolphe Stoclet's collection (Fig. 10) *The Clerical Orgy*, after a sixth-century picture by Zhang Sengyou of the same name, depicting an orgy of Buddhist monks.[127] Although Tang artist Yan Liben was persuaded by resentful Buddhists to paint a picture portraying a Daoist orgy, the Northern Song artist Li Longmian produced copies of both. Waley noted that the painting suggested the work of 'a great master', a piece 'composed in receding space' in which one could 'walk to and fro', mirroring Dong Qichang's comments on *The Drunken Buddhist Monk*, and conjectured that this 'may possibly be Li Lung-mien's original'.[128] Although Waley provided further visual features and comparisons to support his hypothesis, later scholars such as Osvald Sirén refuted this theory, arguing that literary evidence supported it being Yan's *The Drunken Daoist Monk*, a view shared by Xu Beihong.[129] When asked to provide his opinion while reviewing Sirén's book in 1933, Roger Fry at first agreed with Waley. Stating that the work 'may be as Mr. Waley suggests' 'of somewhat later date by a great master in the T'ang style', he eventually accepted it as Yan's *The Drunken Daoist Monk*, although his later Cambridge lectures indicate that he thought it could possibly be a 'Sung copy' of Yan's original.[130] Discussing

126 R. Fry, '*Review of A History of Early Chinese Painting* by Osvald Sirén', *The New Statesman and Nation*, 1933, p. 17.

127 Image from O. Sirén, *A History of Early Chinese Painting*, vol. I, London 1933, pl. 37. Illustrated in Waley, *An Introduction* (n. 116), pl. XXXIV; also in Fry, Last Lectures (n. 104), pl. 242; Sirén, *A History of Early Chinese Painting* (n. 127), p. 60.

128 Waley, *An Introduction* (n. 116), pp. 198-9.

129 Sirén, *A History of Early Chinese Painting* (n. 127), vol. I, pp. 58-60; B. Xu, 'The Paris Chinese Art Exhibition: Brilliance of Antique Paintings', *Art Theory of Beihong*, 1933, Nanjing library (website).

130 Fry, 'Review of *A History of Early Chinese Painting* by Osvald Sirén' (n. 126); Fry, *Last Lectures* (n. 104), pp. 146-7, 227.

Fig. 10 – Attributed to Yan Liben, *The Drunken Daoist Monk*, Tang dynasty (618 – 907), 33.0 x 80.0 cm (Collection of Adolphe Stoclet, Brussels), image from O. Sirén, *A History of Early Chinese Painting*, vol. 1, London, 1933, Pl. 37. Illustrated in A. Waley, *An Introduction to the Study of Chinese Painting*, London, 1958 (First published 1923), Pl. XXXIV; also in R. Fry, *Last Lectures*, Cambridge, 1939, Pl. 242.

身似枯藤心似灰醉
中把筆笑顛哈公
麟津逮僧繇法皴
出兒孫看舞迴
丁丑春御筆再題

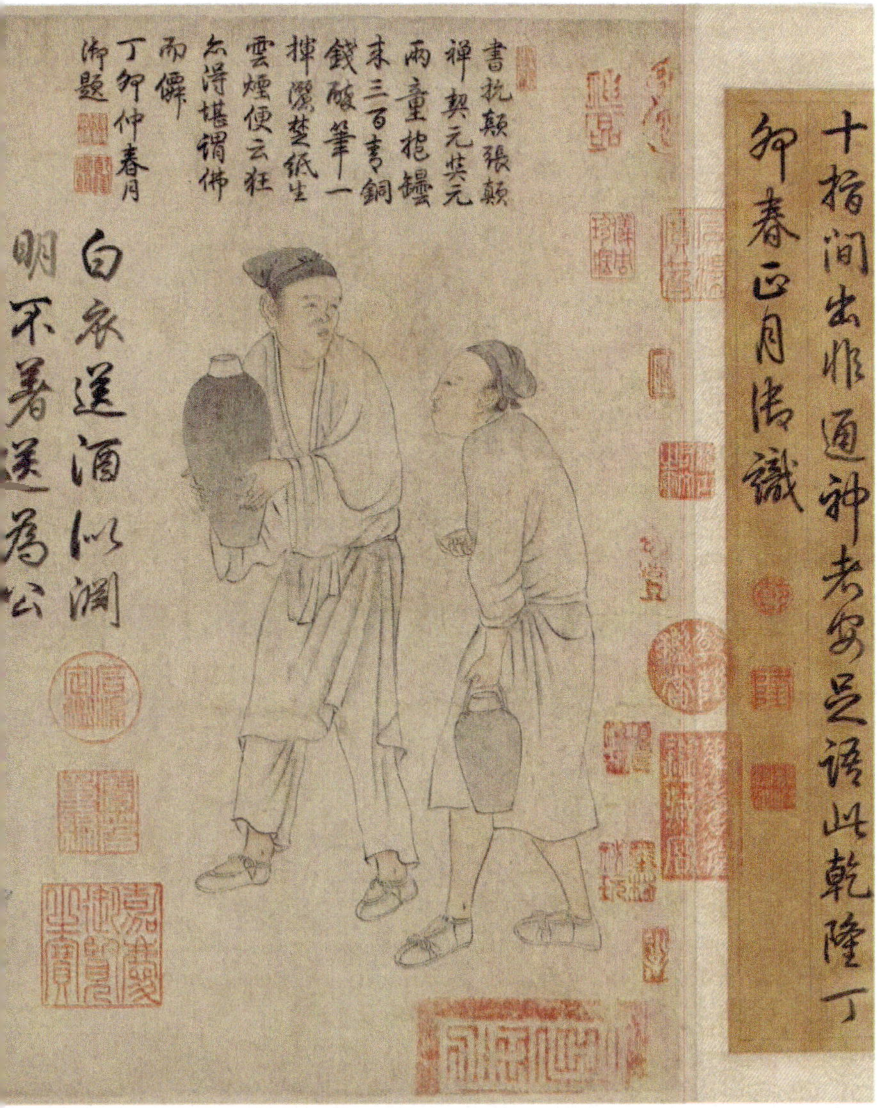

Fig. 11 – Attributed to Li Longmian, *The Drunken Buddhist Monk*, Southern Song dynasty (1127 – 1279), handscroll, ink and colour on paper, 32.5 x 60.8 cm (Freer Gallery of Art, Washington, D.C.).

another painting in the Qianlong collection, identified by its former possessors as Li's *The Drunken Buddhist Monk* (Fig. 11), Waley renamed it *The Calligrapher Huaisu*, drawing a connection to Huaisu's poem. After examining photograph presented to the British Museum by 'Mr. Lu', Waley argued it was not sufficiently 'fine' to be attributed to Li.[131] Due to changing ownership, it would not be until 1981 that a re-examination by Fu Shen attributed it to a Southern Song (1127 – 1279) copy of Li's *The Drunken Buddist Monk*.[132] In comparison to the Stoclet picture (Fig. 10), the difference in style is noticeable. As Qin Xuanfu commented, 'Li is a poet of lines while Yan is a poet of colour, and the fullness of colour stands out as that of Yan'.[133] Although Waley had noticed the 'exquisite colour', his attribution was eventually rejected. This repudiation does not however discredit his methodology. Although his conclusions were not always accurate, his reasoning and process provide valuable insight. The attribution of Chinese paintings is an ongoing process subject to new discoveries, while his unearthing of a relationship with Zhang's original is impressive. Furthermore, while Waley misunderstood the painting's content, he was able to make accurate judgements about its quality and provenance.

Arthur Waley's language was objective and based on original texts, while his personal views were easily lost in his 'almost malicious dryness of manner', and are only to be gleaned from reading between the lines and occasional remarks.[134] Reviewing *An Introduction to the Study of Chinese Painting*, Roger Fry criticized Waley for not sharing 'esthetic experiences' and his refusal to even attempt 'a tentative and preliminary outline of the stylistic

---

131 Probably Lu Qinzhai. Waley, *An Introduction* (n. 116), pp. 199-200.

132 Freer Gallery of Art, 'Object Documentation (F1968.18)', 2010. For detail see *Ōbei shuzō: Chūgoku hōsho meisekishū (Masterpieces of Chinese Calligraphy in American and European Collections)*, vol. I, ed. Y. Nakata and S. Fu, Tokyo 1981, pp. 108 and 145-46, no. 88.

133 X. Qin, 'Read: How to Look at Chinese Painting', CAFA Art Info (website), 2016.

134 R. Fry, 'Review of *An Introduction to the Study of Chinese Painting* by Arthur Waley', *The Burlington Magazine for Connoisseurs*, 44, 1924, pp. 47-48.

development of Chinese painting' for fear of stepping outside the realm of 'definite and precise knowledge'.[135] This criticism was thoroughly unjustified, as Waley's introduction of Wang Wei illustrates. Waley first laid out the history and ideology of the Tang dynasty before approaching Wang's paintings, schematically placing them in a context comprehensible to Western readers. Importantly, Waley stressed how historical events such as the An Lushan Rebellion affected Wang's career and style, how his paintings were perceived in Chinese art history as ancestors of poetical Song (960 – 1279) landscapes, and the significance of his innovative *po mo* (splashed ink) technique.[136]

Arthur Waley's connoisseurship of Chinese art allowed him to correct not only other Western writers such as Herbert Giles, who spoke of Wang Wei as having retired into seclusion when he actually lived as a courtier, but also Chinese writers, who had separated Su Dongpo's comment that 'Wang Wei's pictures were poems and his poems were pictures' from its context.[137] Gei Suzuki expressed a similar view that Su's interpretation of Wang's style had often been misunderstood more than half a century later.[138] While Roger Fry's rhetorical eloquence was persuasive, Waley's scientific inquiry was no less convincing. Concluding that Waley was a strict scientist without aesthetic sense would be inaccurate, however, as he was able to draw upon factual knowledge in order to express subtle aesthetic judgements. This is illustrated in his comments on Yun Shouping's screen (Fig. 12) where Waley describes the manner by which 'the whole beauty' of the work depends on the 'undulating interplay of surfaces and tones' built up by colour to transmit 'the inner essence of a flower's being'.[139] Translating Dong Qichang's inscription on Going up the River for the Spring Festival (Figs. 8 and 9), he remarked that Southern

---

135 Ibid.

136 See Waley, *An Introduction* (n. 116), pp. 91-103 and 141-50.

137 See H. Giles, *An Introduction to the History of Chinese Pictorial Art*, London 1918, p. 56; Waley, *An Introduction* (n. 116), pp. 137-50.

138 Suzuki, *Zhong Guo Hui Hua Shi* (n. 106), p. 85.

Fig. 12 – Yun Shouping (1633 – 1690), screen painted on silk, central portion, 1690 (Collection of Morton Sands), image from *The Year Book of Oriental Art and Culture, Vol. II, Plates*, ed. A. Waley, London, 1925, Pl. 1.

Song copies lacked 'vigour in line', an 'excellent description' of the British Museum version.[140] The 'over-elaboration of detail' in Chinese art was initiated by Wei Xie in the third century, a tendency Waley considered disturbing to the 'united plastic scheme'.[141] However, Waley's analyses and interpretations were not always complete. Acknowledging the influence of European engravings on Chinese paintings of architecture and genre in terms of perspective, he failed to notice their impact on landscape painting.[142] Nevertheless, Waley's publications on Chinese art provided contextual knowledge otherwise inaccessible to Western scholars of the period. Complementing the other Trio members' methodologies, this aspect of Waley's research deserves further recognition as well as appreciation.

Goldsworthy Dickinson: Art and Society

Art, religion, and way of life must be related to economic and technological development. According to Goldsworthy Dickinson, who believed in the composite nature of civilization, it is impossible for a nation to 'pick and choose' between cultural and economic interests.[143] For Dickinson, Chinese art was a direct outcome of the country's societal conditions, and connoisseurship was not only concerned with knowledge of art tradition and literature, but also incorporated by necessity an understanding of government and social structure. Meanwhile, aesthetics would be superficial if the sensitivity aroused by form and style was the only criterion, as art appreciation must be based on external

139 Image from *The Year Book of Oriental Art and Culture, Vol. II, Plates*, ed. A. Waley, London 1925, pl. 1; A. Waley, 'Yün Shou-P'ing Called "Nan-T'ien", 1633 – 1690', *The Year Book of Oriental Art and Culture 1924 – 1925*, London 1925, pp. 1-3. His negligence of Ming and Qing paintings was criticized by William Cohn, an omission Waley attributed to the scarcity and lack of imports in the West. See W. Cohn, *Chinese Painting*, London 1948, p. 87.

140 Waley, 'A Chinese Picture' (n. 121), p. 9.

141 Waley, *An Introduction* (n. 116), pp. 38 and 81.

142 Waley, 'Chinese Philosophy of Art – IX. (Concluded)' (n. 61), pp. 292 and 297-98; for detail on these influences, see M. Sullivan, *The Meeting of Eastern and Western Art*, London 1989, pp. 41-87.

143 Dickinson, 'An Essay on the Civilisations of India, China and Japan' (n. 8), p. 86.

circumstances. Dickinson, 'coloured by a passionately romantic imagination', regarded his work predominantly in the light of its direct social utility.[144] His approach to Chinese art must therefore be understood as part of his ideal of social service, as art for the sake of art or emotion would by contrast appear frivolous to him. For Dickinson, the study of history held value for the human predicament, as obstacles and forces of social progress could be identified and analysed. He endeavoured to discover the optimal path for mankind by offering modifications and alternatives, of which *Letters from John Chinaman* was the 'triumph of his imaginative sympathy'.[145] Amazed at the beauty of its eloquent prose, Roger Fry was positively influenced by it.[146] Dickinson's belief in the 'dignity and beauty' of Chinese tradition, coupled with its capacity to discern beauty and order in nature, anticipated Fry's conception of Chinese art.[147] Acknowledging the social structure within which Chinese art was produced as 'complex and organised' and 'one of the least imperfect' considering its long tradition of continuity, Fry expanded upon Dickinson's ideals by allowing Chinese art to extend beyond non-aesthetic social functions, permitting the artist's sensibility to come fully into play.[148]

For Goldsworthy Dickinson, the antiquity of Chinese art and civilization is proof of the stability of its institutions, maintained by moral relations as dictated by Confucianism. According to Dickinson, the priority of the 'Chinaman' is not to 'strike out a new line for himself' but to revere the past and maintain 'humane and stable relations', as 'society' comes before the 'individual'.[149] This social aspect is reflected in art as the constant revival and imitation of antiquity. Whilst the Confucian 'cult of the past' was

---

144 Fry, 'A Memoir' (n. 27), p. 5.

145 Ibid., pp. 10-12.

146 Fry, *Letters of Roger Fry* (n. 45), vol. I, p. 182.

147 Harding, 'Goldsworthy Lowes Dickinson' (n. 12), p. 32.

148 R. Fry, 'Chinese Art and Architecture', in *China Body & Soul*, ed. E. Hughes, London 1938, pp. 29 and 33.

149 Dickinson, 'Letters from John Chinaman' (n. 6), pp. 12-13.

also acknowledged by Arthur Waley, the 'excessive reverence' for tradition by contemporary Chinese artists was criticized by Roger Fry as the undoing of 'modern Chinese art' that 'never bursts the limits of the inherited formula'.[150]

According to Goldsworthy Dickinson, 'loveliest Nature' produced not only an ancestral lineage of morals, but 'gracious and dignified manners' as well as 'a sense of beauty' in art. Nature is fertile ground for Chinese art, giving it a peculiar sensitivity and insight. The separation of art and nature, Dickinson argued, had contributed to the degeneration of the West, a fact reflected in its 'superfluous', fatuous, and banal art.[151] For Dickinson, the Chinese adherence to the soil sowed by their ancestors produced in artists an unmediated sensitivity to the world around them. This sensitivity was reflected in landscape painting, where 'beautiful' and 'real' nature was contemplated by humble observers.[152] Nature was sympathetic to mankind, and the proximity to it made Chinese art humane. For Dickinson's Chinaman, to feel, understand and express 'all that is lovely in Nature' was 'a sufficient end' in itself.[153] This contrasted with Arthur Waley's perspective, in which nature was first and foremost a source of inspiration. The Chinese adoration of nature bordered on 'religious fervour' and transformed into 'romantic aestheticism', culminating in *shan shui* (mountain and water) landscapes. Waley explained that the Chinese character *xian* (holy) is written with the elements 'man' and 'mountain', associating the divine with landscape. The Daoist ideal and mood offered by scenery prompted the 'Mountain Man' to seek spiritual satisfaction in landscape painting, while nature offered the ideal subject.[154] For Roger Fry, nature presented natural forms to be imitated by

---

150 Waley, An Introduction (n. 116), pp. 18-19; R. Fry, 'Some Aspects of Chinese Art', *Transformations*, New York 1968, p. 70.

151 Dickinson, 'Letters from John Chinaman' (n. 6), pp. 18-23.

152 Dickinson, 'An Essay on the Civilisations of India, China and Japan' (n. 8), p. 66.

153 Dickinson, 'Letters from John Chinaman' (n. 6), pp. 27-8.

154 Waley, *An Introduction* (n. 116), p. 137.

artists to produce specific emotional states.[155] Agreeing with Waley that cultured men in Chinese bureaucracy desired to escape social life 'to live free and fearless in the isolation of the hills', Fry considered Chinese landscape painting a product of the imaginative mind which offered 'a source of spiritual satisfaction'.[156]

The Cambridge Trio: Aesthetics, Knowledge and Society

Although the members of the Cambridge Trio had different approaches, their discrepancies should not be magnified. Roger Fry's neglect of context was not deliberate but rather a compromise. As he acknowledged, an emphasis on the cultural rather than aesthetic values of Oriental objects is prudent, since 'it is generally through cultural policies that we can get fresh perspectives of esthetic values'; aesthetic principles can only be reached through the thorough investigation of cultural aspects.[157] This concept was repeated in his review of *The Eumorfopoulos Collection*, in which he challenged Laurence Binyon's ignorance of dates, arguing that the desire for 'an ordered sequence' is natural to gain 'a sense of the tides of the spiritual life of mankind', although 'aesthetic reactions' should from time to time be given free rein 'without any conditioning circumstances'.[158] Focused on historical truth, Arthur Waley was alert to context, as evidenced by his criticism of Wei dynasty (386 – 534) painters who failed to bring figures into 'plastic relation' with the scene.[159] Indeed, his focus on the written word places him in close relation to authentic Chinese scholarship, finding sympathy with Goldsworthy Dickinson's Chinaman who stated that 'in China letters are respected not merely to a degree but in a sense which must seem, I think, to you unintelligible and overstrained'.[160] As Oscar

155 Fry, 'An Essay in Aesthetics' (n. 11), pp. 36-8.

156 Fry, 'Chinese Art and Architecture' (n. 148), pp. 36-7.

157 R. Fry, 'Oriental Art', *Nation and Athenaeum*, 1925, p. 650.

158 R. Fry, 'Chinese Frescoes', *Nation and Athenaeum*, 1927, pp. 751-2.

159 Waley, An Introduction (n. 116), p. 139.

160 Dickinson, 'Letters from John Chinaman' (n. 6), p. 27.

Browning remarked, 'no Cambridge man can endure' that 'a man should know anything outside his own subject'.[161] Waley's focus on objective facts should thus be viewed as a rigorous scholarly attitude, restricting himself to his field of specialization. As Fry admitted, Waley's 'literary materials', supported by his 'linguistic powers', were vital for the history of Chinese painting, and that confining himself to what he was 'pre-eminently fitted' for was perhaps a wise decision.[162]

As evidenced by their shared affection for animals represented in Chinese art, an interest in aesthetics connected Roger Fry and Arthur Waley. Although the human figure is generally considered the most important artistic subject matter, Fry suggested that animals have historically served as the first objects of representation, as is found with 'every modern child'.[163] For Fry, art as an expression of the imaginative life is observed in the carefree drawing of children, whose mental images conceived animals and humans as being of equal importance.[164] It is a 'purely native and untouched art'.[165] The Chinese contribution to 'our spiritual life' could be detected precisely in the artists' depictions of animals.[166] Fry noted that the contrast between the European anthropocentric view and the Chinese perspective, where man is one of the many manifestations of divine energy, had been illustrated earlier by Raphael Petrucci.[167] While Europeans inherited 'a peculiar arrogance', fixing early and indelibly an 'anthropocentric illusion' in their minds, Chinese artists never narrowly focused their attention on their own

161 Dickinson, *The Autobiography of G. Lowes Dickinson and Other Unpublished Writings* (n. 16), p. 65.

162 Fry, 'Review of *An Introduction to the Study of Chinese Painting* by Arthur Waley' (n. 134), p. 8.

163 R. Fry, 'Introduction', in H. d'Ardenne de Tizac, *Animals in Chinese Art: A Collection of Examples*, London and Paris 1923, p. 1.

164 Fry, 'An Essay in Aesthetics' (n. 11), p. 20.

165 R. Fry, 'Children's Drawings', The Papers of Roger Eliot Fry, King's College Archive, REF/1/23, p. 8. See also R. Fry, 'Children's Drawings', *The Burlington Magazine for Connoisseurs*, 30 (171), 1917, pp. 225-27 and 231.

166 Fry, 'Some Aspects of Chinese Art' (n. 150), p. 77.

167 Fry. 'Review of *La philosophie de la nature dans l'art d'Extrême-Orient* by Raphael Petrucci' (n. 82), pp. 106-7.

species, giving significance to animal and plant forms.[168] For Fry, the 'extraordinary vitality of these creatures' often exhibited in Chinese art does not show preconceived human qualities, bestowing animals with a 'unique and strangely unapproachable life' of their own.[169] In his letter to Gerald Brenan, he marvelled at the Chinese imagination in which *rien ne tire à conséquence*, even in religion.[170] The condition of mind in which these works were created was a state of detachment, 'neither so passionate nor so serious', connected with 'happy disinterestedness'.[171] That an object of art 'subserving the imaginative life' is adapted for 'disinterested intensity of contemplation' so that 'responsive action' could be cut off is key for the judgement of taste.[172] Should the imaginative life of the artist be spared imperative immediate action and its emotional values purified, then Chinese art would represent the apex of free imagination, engaging in playful representational work, such as non-anthropomorphic animal forms. Chinese artists do not take the world or themselves too seriously, Fry argued, so they 'can afford to play' with 'the offspring' of imagination, creating an 'art of freedom and gaiety'.[173] Fry noted this attitude with some frequency in animal-shaped Zhou bronzes, and later reappeared in the 'purely picturesque and external curiosity' of Song paintings that 'modern European art habitually displays'.[174] This 'playfulness and detachment' is 'inherent in the Chinese spirit'.[175] The emotional resonance of representation is central to this argument.[176]

Reviewing the 1923 publication *Animals in Chinese Art*, a com-

---

168 Fry, 'Some Aspects of Chinese Art' (n. 150), p. 77.

169 Fry, 'Introduction', in *Animals in Chinese Art: A Collection of Examples* (n. 163), 1923, p. 1.

170 Fry, *Letters of Roger Fry* (n. 45), vol. II, p. 691.

171 Fry, 'Introduction', in *Animals in Chinese Art: A Collection of Examples* (n. 163), p. 2.

172 Fry, 'An Essay in Aesthetics' (n. 11), p. 29.

173 D. Laing, *Roger Fry: An Annotated Bibliography of the Published Writings*, New York and London 1979, p. 48.

174 Fry, 'Some Aspects of Chinese Art' (n. 150), pp. 78-79.

175 Fry, 'Introduction', in *Animals in Chinese Art: A Collection of Examples* (n. 163), p. 3.

176 R. Fry, 'The Eumorfopoulos Collection', *Nation and Athenaeum*, 1928, pp. 652-53.

Fig. 13 – *Jar in the Shape of an Owl*, Zhou dynasty (1046 – 256 BC), earthenware, H. 16.2 cm (Musée Cernuschi, Paris), image from H. d'Ardenne de Tizac, *Animals in Chinese Art: A Collection of Examples*, London and Paris, 1923, Pl. II B.

pilation of examples from public and private collections, Arthur Waley marvelled at the 'archaeological interest' and 'great intrinsic beauty' of the objects. Like Roger Fry, Waley viewed the Chinese attitude towards animals as far from 'sentimental', a belief derived from the 'primitive contact with the beasts' and the Buddhist teaching that 'the soul of a grasshopper may once have inhabited the body of a king'.[177] Of the *Jar in the Form of an Owl* (Fig. 13), Waley quoted Fry's description of 'an owl sitting, "warming his five wits", with shoulders hunched and feathers puffed'.[178] Unusually, he enthusiastically extolled his friend's aesthetic approach as 'the more difficult course' since 'it is always easier to talk of archaeology than of art'.[179] Lamenting that Henri d'Ardenne de Tizac had failed to offer sufficient visual descriptions in the publication, and noting that certain omissions of archaeological information and bibliography were 'of relatively small importance', Waley portrayed himself as a true aesthetician.[180]

As illustrated by their treatments of Han art, the approaches of Roger Fry and Arthur Waley were often complementary. Waley considered it natural that upon seeing illustrations of Han tomb reliefs of dancing figures (Fig. 14) and imaginative divinities (Fig. 15), one would understand the kind of 'life and thought' people had in this period.[181] The context in which these pictures occurred and their respective literature serve as evidence to 'refute M. Grousset's assertion that but for Buddhist influences Chinese painting would never have existed'.[182] In order to provide richer

177 A. Waley, 'Animals in Chinese Art', *The Burlington Magazine for Connoisseurs*, 42 (242), 1923, pp. 215-16 (215).

178 Image from H. d'Ardenne de Tizac, *Animals in Chinese Art: A Collection of Examples*, London and Paris 1923, pl. II B; Fry, 'Some Aspects of Chinese Art' (n. 150), p. 78.

179 Waley, 'Animals in Chinese Art' (n. 163), p. 215.

180 Ibid., p. 216.

181 Images from *Han Tomb Art of West China: A Collection of First- and Second-Century Reliefs*, ed. R. Rudolph and Y. Wen, Berkeley and Los Angeles 1951, pl. 77. Illustrated in A. Waley, 'Life Under the Han Dynasty', *History Today*, 1953, pl. 4 and n. 205, pl. 95. Waley, 'Life Under the Han Dynasty'(n. 181), pp. 89-98.

182 Waley, *An Introduction* (n. 116), p. 31.

Fig. 14 – *A Festive Scene*, Han dynasty (206 BC – AD 220), relief on brick and tile, 46.0 x 42.0 cm (Private collection, Chengdu), image from *Han Tomb Art of West China: A Collection of First- and Second-Century Reliefs*, ed. R. Rudolph and Y. Wen, Berkeley and Los Angeles, 1951, Pl. 77.
Illustrated in A. Waley, 'Life Under the Han Dynasty', *History Today*, 1953, Pl. 4.

Fig. 15 – *A Birdlike Creature with Human Face*, Han dynasty (206 BC – AD 220), relief on brick and tile, 31.0 x 40.5 cm (Private collection, Chengdu), image from *Han Tomb Art of West China: A Collection of First- and Second-Century Reliefs*, ed. R. Rudolph and Y. Wen, Berkeley and Los Angeles, 1951, Pl. 95.

Fig. 16 – *Attempted Assassination*, Han dynasty (206 BC – AD 220), engraved stone (Musée Guimet, Paris), image from R. Fry, *Last Lectures*, Cambridge, 1939, Pl. 193.

and more accurate contextual knowledge for the 1951 'descriptive catalogue' *Han Tomb Art of West China*, a compilation of examples from Sichuan, Waley provided the 'full details' of geography, ethnicity, government, religious beliefs and commerce, concluding that its makers led peaceful lives and that the 'luxuriant' and 'tropical' feel of the period could be attributed to Indian influence in the earlier Kingdom of Chu (ca. 1030 – 223 BC).[183] Such conclusions were important, as prior to the discovery of Han pictures in Sichuan, stone rubbings from east China were considered the only paintings of the period.[184] Meanwhile, Fry captured the spirit of the period through formalist analysis. With its tendency to replace plastic form with linear and flat design, Han art marked the 'real beginning' of Chinese painting, where lines and intervals gave rise to artistic modernity. Echoing Fry, Michael Sullivan would later rely on the 'extraordinary abstraction' of visual quality to ascertain the birth of indigenous Chinese landscape painting. Citing 'symbolic forms based on abstract linear rhythms' that were 'inherently Chinese' and which could be traced to Taotie patterns on Shang bronzes, Sullivan rejected the commonly-suggested Near Eastern origin.[185] That these Han tomb paintings marked early renderings of space and exhibited the beginnings of early brushwork would also later be accepted by James Cahill in his lectures.[186]

As Roger Fry noted, the stone rubbing from Shandong (Fig. 16) depicting an assassination attempt on the Qin Emperor showed a 'perfect ease of representation' free from 'struggle'; its perspective so 'slight and the sense of intervals so sure that the

---

183 Waley, 'Life Under the Han Dynasty' (n. 180), p. 90; Waley, *An Introduction* (n. 116), pp. 22-23.

184 *Han Tomb Art of West China: A Collection of First- and Second-Century Reliefs* (n. 181), p. 3.

185 M. Sullivan, 'On the Origin of Landscape Representation in Chinese Art', *Archives of the Chinese Art Society of America*, 7, 1953, pp. 59 and 63; A. Soper, 'Early Chinese Landscape Painting', *The Art Bulletin*, 23 (2), 1941, p. 147. For detail see O. Sirén, *Histoire des arts anciens de la Chine*, vol. II, Paris and Brussels 1929.

186 J. Cahill, 'Lecture 2 – Han Painting and Pictorial Designs', *A Pure and Remote View: Visualizing Early Chinese Landscape Painting* (video), 1:03 hour.

total effect of pattern impresses us at once'.[187] The primary concern of 'illustration' often displays the artist's incredible 'pictorial understanding' as seen in a rudimentary Han draughtsman painting (Fig. 17), where 'the simplicity of the contour and its power to suggesting volume' is what 'reminds one of Giotto'.[188] Although Han reliefs from east China had comparatively more text than their counterparts from the western region of the country, Fry deliberately sketched contextual information light-heartedly while Arthur Waley did the opposite and overlooked the unique visual qualities of Han painting as well as its art-historical significance.[189] This study was not lost on future generations of art historians. Wu Hung's writing on the same relief (Fig. 16) emphasized regional styles of Han pictorial art and called for new models to interpret chronological and geographical developments.[190] Discussing the interrelated nature of the psychological and plastic aspects of graphic art, Fry referred to 'certain early Chinese paintings' as 'religious caricature' with 'psychological volumes'.[191] This easy representation of emotion, as illustrated in the Arhat by Guan Xiu (Fig. 18), appealed to Fry.[192] Guan's unusual 'individual style', powerful in its suggestion of plastic relief, was 'akin to Western pictorial ideas', an opinion shared by Waley, who viewed the 'purely plastic' work of the 'first great individual painter' as beneficial for many future generations of European students.[193]

Roger Fry and Arthur Waley's complementary nature is also displayed in their writings on *Taizong's Charger* (Fig. 19).[194] As both

---

187 Image from Fry, *Last Lectures* (n. 104), pl. 193.

188 Image from Fry, *Last Lectures* (n. 104), pl. 195; Fry, *Last Lectures* (n. 104), pp. 130-31.

189 Waley, 'Life Under the Han Dynasty' (n. 180), p. 95.

190 H. Wu, *The Wu Liang Shrine: The Ideology of Early Chinese Pictorial Art*, Stanford 1989, pp. 53-54.

191 Fry, 'Some Questions in Esthetics' (n. 90), p. 11.

192 Image from Waley, *An Introduction* (n. 116), pl. XXXI. Illustrated in Fry, *Last Lectures* (n. 104), pl. 243.

193 Fry, *Last Lectures* (n. 104), pp. 147-8; Waley, *An Introduction* (n. 116), p. 167.

194 Illustrated in Fry, *Last Lectures* (n. 104), pl. 231.

Fig. 17 – *Two Heads* (from Hall of Zhu Wei, Jinxiang, Shandong), Han dynasty (206 BC – AD 220), image from R. Fry, *Last Lectures*, Cambridge, 1939, Pl. 195.

Fig. 18 – Attributed to Guan Xiu, *Arhat*, The Five dynasties (907 – 960), 127.3 x 66.0 cm (Collection of Baron Takahashi, Tokyo), image from A. Waley, *An Introduction to the Study of Chinese Painting*, London, 1958 (First published 1923), Pl. XXXI. Illustrated in R. Fry, *Last Lectures*, Cambridge, 1939, Pl. 243.

Fig. 19 – *Taizong's Charger*, 649, limestone, H. 172.7 cm, L. 207.0 cm, W. 43.2 cm (University of Pennsylvania Museum of Archaeology and Anthropology, Philadelphia). Illustrated in R. Fry, *Last Lectures*, Cambridge, 1939, Pl. 231.

were likely to have encountered the work from the same source, an article by Charles Bishop in *The Museum Journal* in 1918, and had seen casts of the original at the British Museum, their differing yet compatible approaches can be straightforwardly compared. While Waley's priority was to present untranslated Chinese sources and to correct mistakes of previous scholars, Fry emphasized the 'exuberant energy and self-confidence' of Tang art.[195] Referring to *Li Dai Ming Hua Ji*, Waley argued that the reliefs were based on drawings by Yan Liben instead of You Jingshu, as had been suggested in a 1918 *Museum Journal* article.[196] As confirmed by You's inscriptions on slabs in the ancestral shrine of Taizong, and as recounted in *Xin Tang Shu (New Tang History)*, the man in 'Tartar costume' pulling an arrow from the horse's breast should actually portray the Chinese general Qiu Xinggong.[197] Supported by a Japanese source that confirmed the 'supposedly Tartar costume' was typical of Tang military attire, Waley's attribution continues to be referenced to this day.[198] Commenting on the same artwork, Fry identified the 'monumental gravity and solidity' as the 'straining energy' underlying its stillness. The 'conscious and learned' artist, likely recognized as such given his selection for the emperor's tomb, expertly conveyed the idea of high relief suggesting 'mass and force' without contradicting its 'architectural function'.[199] As Fry's description suggests, the identity of the creator and subject of an artwork were less important than the period's spirit expressed by mass, volume and design.

---

195 A. Waley, 'T'ai Tsung's Six Chargers', *The Burlington Magazine for Connoisseurs*, 43, 1923, pp. 117-18; Fry, *Last Lectures* (n. 104), pp. 142-43.

196 See C. Bishop, 'The Horses of T'ang T'ai-Tsung, of the Antecedents of the Chinese Horse', *The Museum Journal*, Philadelphia 1918, p. 266.

197 Official history of the Tang dynasty, compiled by Northern Song scholars led by Ouyang Xiu and Song Qi.

198 Waley, 'T'ai Tsung's Six Chargers' (n. 195), p. 118; for recent citations of Waley, see X. Zhou, 'The Mausoleum of Emperor Tang Taizong', Sino-Platonic Papers, 187, 2009, pp. 25 and 42, and P. Karetzky, *Court Art of the Tang*, London 1996, pp. 20-21.

199 Fry, *Last Lectures* (n. 104), p. 143.

Accessibility, Classic Spirit and Modernity

The Accessibility of Chinese Art

At a time when most Western viewers were content with 'trifling bibelots' and chinoiseries and considered Chinese objects strange with unintelligible symbols, the pioneering vision of the Cambridge Trio played a pivotal role in changing public opinion. As Roger Fry remarked, 'Chinese art is in reality extremely accessible to European sensibility' if one could approach it with the same 'attentive passivity' as one might cultivate before an Italian Renaissance masterpiece or a Gothic or Romanesque sculpture.[200] What is more, Chinese literature and ordinary countryside architecture are fundamentally similar to those of Europe and belong to the 'classic tradition'.[201] Fry gave examples of European artists such as Botticelli and Ingres whose works rely on linear schemes and who were 'essentially Chinese'.[202] Comparing a Tang Bhikshu statue (Fig. 20) with the relief figures of Giotto's Campanile (Fig. 21), Fry noted that both were 'essentially plastic' and 'free of the third dimension', and yet while the Giotto departs from the simple polyhedron, as evidenced by the torso of the seated woman whose plane of the breast changes with 'uniform direction', there is a marked tendency towards a roundness of form in keeping with Chinese tendencies, with the basic schema manifested by the shoulders and chest of the figure that scarcely depart 'from the abstract egg-shape which permeates almost every part of the design'.[203] The Chinese sense of linear scheme is again noticed in the drapery of the statue, which envelopes the figure in simple linear rhythms, accentuating the round contour of the whole.[204] For Fry, Chinese religious art

---

200 R. Fry, 'Chinese Art', *Burlington Magazine Monographs*, London 1925, pp. 1-4.

201 Fry, 'Chinese Art and Architecture' (n. 148), pp. 42-43.

202 Fry, 'Chinese Art' (n. 200), pp. 2-3. For such studies, see G. Soulier, *Les influences orientales dans la peinture toscane*, Paris 1924.

203 Images from R. Fry, Transformations, New York 1968, pls. XIV and XIII.

204 Fry, 'Some Aspects of Chinese Art' (n. 150), pp. 75-76.

Fig. 20 – *Stone Sculpture of Bhikshu*,
Tang dynasty (618 – 907), image from R. Fry, *Transformations*,
New York, 1968, Pl. XIV.

Fig. 21 – Italian sculptor influenced by Giotto, *The Art of Weaving*, mid-14th century, relief on Campanile, Florence, image from R. Fry, *Transformations*, New York, 1968, Pl. XIII.

offered no obstacle to an audience unfamiliar with Avalokatesvara, Amidha or Arhat.[205]

Arthur Waley shared Roger Fry's view on the essential accessibility of Chinese art, albeit through the prism of literature. Sometimes considered 'a new English poet', Waley's translations connected Chinese poetry with its modern European counterparts.[206] For the English public who were familiar with Chinese landscape scrolls, literary and visual sources worked together to prepare them for Chinese art.[207] Presenting indigenous material in an approachable manner, Waley considered Chinese art accessible as long as a framework of art history, incorporating provenance and literature similar to that of European art, could be established.

Analysing Taotie patterns, Arthur Waley noted that they had never been subjected to 'the same kind of analysis' as Western designs. Furthermore, he argued that the 'technical nomenclature' of these ritual vessels would only be of interest if the audience was able to study the details of the contexts in which they were used.[208] Citing recent archaeological discoveries in Mongolia, Waley suggested a possible Siberian origin. Confirming that *Lüshi Chunqiu (Discourse of Lü Buwei)* contains the earliest known literary descriptions of Taotie patterns, a zoomorphic motif commonly found on ancient Chinese bronze, Waley translated the original text as 'on Chou vessels there was put a t'ao-t'ieh with a head, but no body', a reference which would have been useful to previous scholars.[209] Illustrated in several public and private collections (Figs. 22 and 23), Waley stated that this 'rare' Taotie pattern symbolized the 'acquisitive State'.[210] Correcting the Japanese

205 Fry, 'Chinese Art' (n. 200), p. 1.

206 'He Never Went to China – A Portrait of Arthur Waley' (n. 9), pp. 139-40.

207 Laurence, *Lily Briscoe's Chinese Eyes* (n. 10), pp. 305-6.

208 A. Waley and W. Yetts, 'The T'ao-t'ieh', *The Burlington Magazine for Connoisseurs*, 48 (275), 1926, pp. 104-8.

209 Compiled ca. 239 BC.

210 Image from *Burlington Magazine Monographs*, London, 1925, Bronzes – pl. 5A.

Fig. 22 – *You*, late Shang dynasty (ca. 1550 – 1050 BC), bronze, H. 30.5 cm (Collection of Baron Sumitomo, Tokyo), image from *Burlington Magazine Monographs*, London, 1925, Bronzes – Pl. 5A.

Fig. 23 – *You Vessel in the Shape of a Feline*, late Shang dynasty (ca. 1550 – 1050 BC), bronze, H. 35.2 cm, L. 23.6 cm, W. 23.3 cm (Musée Cernuschi, Paris).

scholarly belief that this type of bronze was unknown to Chinese literature, and that of Ernst Voretzsch, who thought that it originated during the Qin dynasty (221 – 206 BC), Waley confirmed its mention in early local writings and its Zhou design. The theory that the term Taotie was used to describe monsters on Chinese bronzes from Song onwards, as suggested in the *Burlington Magazine Monograph*, was also mistaken.[211] Waley suggested that, based on written history, the importation of designs in Chinese art had happened as early as the Han dynasty, thus 'there is no reason not to suppose' that the Taotie pattern produced 'before definite history begins' was of foreign origin.[212] Overemphasizing literary evidence has its drawbacks as written records can be inaccurate and subjective. Waley did not realize that the first occurrence of the word Taotie was in *Zuo Zhuan (Commentary of Zuo)*,[213] where the term was used to describe gluttony, before being associated with bronze in the *Discourse of Lü Buwei*.[214] As later archaeological discoveries would confirm, this type of pattern is of Shang design, predating its appearance in literature.[215] Further excavations would trace the prototype of Taotie to a mask motif on pottery from the Hemudu (5500 – 3300 BC) period, a local Neolithic culture in the lower reach of the Yangzi river.[216] This mask pattern survived in Liangzhu (3400 – 2250 BC) jade decorations and was transformed into various Taotie patterns on Shang and Zhou bronzes, further indicating its indigenous origin.[217] Although its association with bronze appears in early texts, it was the Song scholars of *jin shi xue* (epigraphy) who established the norm of using Taotie to describe this design, while the original name used during Shang and Zhou

211 For detail see W. Yetts, 'Bronzes', *Burlington Magazine Monographs*, London, 1925, p. 43.

212 Waley and Yetts, 'The T'ao-t'ieh' (n. 208), p. 107.

213 By Zuo Qiuming, Spring and Autumn period (770 – 476 BC).

214 On the use of 'Tatoie' to describe gluttony, see 'Wen Gong Shi Ba Nian', *Zuo Zhuan* ('The Eighteenth Year of Weng Gong', *Commentary of Zuo*).

215 '*You* Vessels in the Shape of a Feline', *Musée Cernuschi* (website), Object No. M.C. 6155.

216 H. Wu, *Monumentality in Early Chinese Art and Architecture*, Stanford 1995, p. 32.

217 J. Rawson, *Ancient China: Art and Archaeology*, London 1980, pp. 36-40 and 70-79.

remains unknown.[218] Waley, however, should not be accused of negligence. Lacking access to archaeological information, he could not have made a cross-material comparison or discussed the stylistic development of this pattern. As Roger Fry noted, the Western understanding of Chinese art grew rapidly when early objects became readily available, and thus Waley's association of Taotie with the *Discourse of Lü Buwei* was already a substantial step that furthered Western knowledge.[219]

Despite their exotic nature and indiscernible origin, Roger Fry believed that Taotie patterns and Chinese bronzes were accessible to Western audiences because of their formal aspects. This exotic quality had 'favourable appeal', having been produced by people who were 'polite', 'traditional' and 'sophisticated', near to 'our own ways of living and feeling'. For Fry, there was something 'safe and comfortable' about Chinese art, so that even the 'grinning monster's faces' (Taotie) could 'fit so comfortably into our own rooms'.[220] Neither referencing literary sources nor interrogating symbolic meanings, he adhered to formal features by paying attention to the 'underlying vigour' of Zhou bronzes that presented a 'singular tact and reticence' representative of the 'most distinguished good manners'. The 'variety and flexibility' of curves leading up to the lip, coupled with 'firmness' of the base, and the relief 'monster's head (the T'ao-t'ieh)' as exhibited in this 'specimen of Chou craftsmanship' (Fig. 24) show 'a complete plastic idea' expressed with 'perfect assurance and ease'.[221] Although Fry failed to notice the Shang date of the object, his primary concern was how the Taotie design fit into

---

218 On the Song scholars, see *Kao Gu Tu (Archaeology Icon)*, by Lü Dalin, compiled in the Northern Song period, Chapter One, and Z. Bian, X. Zhou and Y. Shi, *Zhongguo Gongyi Meishushi (History of Chinese Works of Art)*, Beijing 2008. On the original name, see S. Allan, 'The Taotie Motif on Early Chinese Ritual Bronzes', in *The Zoomorphic Imagination in Chinese Art and Culture*, ed. J. Silbergeld and E. Wang, Honolulu 2016, p.27.

219 Fry, 'Chinese Bronzes at Messrs. Yamanaka's' (n. 7), p. 494.

220 Ibid.

221 Image from R. Fry, *Transformations*, New York 1968, pl. XI, as *Bronze Sacrificial Vessel, Chou Dynasty*; Fry, 'Some Aspects of Chinese Art' (n. 150), pp. 70-1.

Fig. 24 – *Pou*, late Shang dynasty (12th – 11th century BC) (Collection of Takeuchi, Tokyo), image from R. Fry, *Transformations*, New York, 1968, Pl. XI, as *Bronze Sacrificial Vessel, Chou Dynasty*.

the linear and plastic treatment of the vessel.[222] For Fry, it was 'the degree of development' of art rather than 'the race or the religion that produced it' that was essential.[223]

The opinion that Chinese art and civilization were accessible to the West was shared by Goldsworthy Dickinson, who claimed that China was the 'most peaceful' and 'law-abiding' nation on earth. For him, rebellion and violence were only proofs of the intensity and brutality of foreign provocations.[224] Despite the Boxer Rebellion and Opium Wars, Dickinson defended the Chinese people, suggesting that the majority of its population were ignorant of the revolution's drivers, merely welcoming it as a relief from tax payment.[225] After reading Arthur Waley's translations of Chinese poems, Roger Fry reached the same conclusion, referring to the 'old Chinese bureaucrats of the Han and T'ang periods' as 'truly civilized', stating that they would be considered 'sentimental humanitarians' today.[226] According to Dickinson, the lack of 'national sentiment' was embedded in a social organization based on family and village rather than central government.[227] Dickinson's passionate tone not only shocked Western readers out of their 'self-complacent sense of superiority', but also revealed to the Chinese the European appreciation of the 'dignity and beauty' of Chinese tradition.[228] While less emotional, the impassioned voice of Waley was equally effective. Publishing what is sometimes considered the sequel to Dickinson's *Letters from John Chinaman*, *The Opium War Through Chinese Eyes*, Waley included translations and compilations of Chinese material, particularly intimate documents such as

---

222 See comparative example in R. Bagley, *Ancient Chinese Bronzes in the Arthur M. Sackler Collections, vol. I, Shang Ritual Bronzes in the Arthur M. Sackler Collections*, Washington, D.C. 1987, pl. 57.

223 Fry, 'Introduction' (n. 91), in *Discourses*, p. XIII.

224 Dickinson, 'Letters from John Chinaman' (n. 6), p. 41.

225 Dickinson, 'An Essay on the Civilisations of India, China and Japan' (n. 8), p. 74.

226 Fry, *Letters of Roger Fry* (n. 45), vol. II, p. 418.

227 Dickinson, 'An Essay on the Civilisations of India, China and Japan' (n. 8), p. 74.

228 Fry, 'A Memoir' (n. 27), pp. 13-14.

diaries, autobiographies and confessions of personalities like Commissioner Lin Zexu.[229] Having often been omitted by previous European scholars, these accounts offered a Chinese experience of the war for Western readers.[230] Presenting hard facts in an objective tone, Waley was able to alter the prejudiced view of his countrymen. Although some of his contemporaries doubted that China would have been 'in a more advantageous position' in terms of modernization and industrialization, 'respect' for Commissioner Lin increased.[231] Waley was applauded for giving Western audiences 'the basic stuff of history in the humanistic sense of experience', which was a core belief that he shared with Dickinson, whose earlier writing 'sowed the seeds of [Waley's] achievement'.[232]

For Goldsworthy Dickinson, the accessibility of Chinese art was natural given the character of its civilization and people. When he eventually travelled to Asia, Dickinson noted the 'profound gulf' between Asian countries, and yet a Chinese national is 'not so unlike an Englishman',[233] 'a kind of English with sensitiveness and imagination'.[234] The 'dominant note' of China is 'humanity', understood as the 'secularism' of life's attitude in which 'Mankind' is the centre of the universe, with ancestor worship as the core of the system. It was this 'common humanity' that became the basis for Tong Qingsheng's study on global civilization.[235] For Dickinson, the same humanity and secularism were expressed in Chinese art, which was 'through

---

229 Harding, 'Goldsworthy Lowes Dickinson' (n. 12), p. 38.

230 A. Waley, *The Opium War Through Chinese Eyes*, London, 1958, pp. 7-8.

231 J. Cheng, 'Review of *The Opium War Through Chinese Eyes* by Arthur Waley', *Pacific Affairs*, 33 (1), 1960, pp. 68-9.

232 J. Fairbank, 'Review of *The Opium War through Chinese Eyes* by Arthur Waley', *Far Eastern Survey*, 28 (10), 1959, pp. 159-60; Laurence, *Lily Briscoe's Chinese Eyes* (n. 10), p. 306.

233 Dickinson, 'An Essay on the Civilisations of India, China and Japan' (n. 8), p. 46.

234 Forster, *Goldsworthy Lowes Dickinson* (n. 15), p. 148.

235 Q. Tong, 'Towards a Common Civilization: G. Lowes Dickinson, China, and Global Humanism', *Canadian Review of Comparative Literature*, 6, 2014, pp. 156-73.

Fig. 25 – *Mirror*, Han dynasty (206 BC – AD 220), bronze, D. 17.8 cm, image from R. Fry, 'Some Chinese Antiquities', *The Burlington Magazine for Connoisseurs*, 43 (249), 1923, Pl. I B.

Fig. 26 – *Mirror*, Han dynasty (206 BC – AD 220), bronze, D. 21.6 cm, image from R. Fry, 'Some Chinese Antiquities', *The Burlington Magazine for Connoisseurs*, 43 (249), 1923, Pl. I C.

and through human'. Resonating with the 'pathos and gaiety' of human life as well as the 'beauty and grandeur' of nature, Dickinson suggested that it is the kind of art that Romans or Englishmen 'might have produced' had they the 'aesthetic genius'.[236] The spiritual forces that both Dickinson and Fry opposed were not completely absent in Chinese art. Writing of two Han mirrors (Fig. 25, Fig. 26) in the Yamanaka collection, Fry saw 'spiritual forces' that have 'always been latent in humanity' and which prompted a degradation of taste as evidenced by the lack of sensitivity.[237] It was through the formal aspects of their work that one can discover the inner spirit of the Chinese artists, which is essentially human.

The Classic Spirit of Chinese Art

A key element of Roger Fry's aesthetics was the notion of classicism derived from Maurice Denis's definition of formal order and unity of design.[238] Cut off from 'practical responses to sensations of ordinary life', classical art does not rely upon 'associated ideas' but rather records 'a positive and disinterestedly passionate state of mind' while communicating 'a new and otherwise unattainable experience'.[239] Unbound and spontaneous without the pressure to represent or depict, emanating an atmosphere with which the viewer can sympathize, the same classic spirit appeared in French post-impressionism and in Chinese art, according to Fry. The free and contemplative classic spirit, he suggested, is one and the same as the 'playfulness and detachment' inherent in the Chinese frame of mind.[240]

---

236 Dickinson, 'An Essay on the Civilisations of India, China and Japan' (n. 8), pp. 48-66.

237 Image from R. Fry, 'Some Chinese Antiquities', *The Burlington Magazine for Connoisseurs*, 43 (249), 1923, p. 281, pls. I B and I C. See M. Denis, 'Cézanne', *The Burlington Magazine for Connoisseurs*, transl. R. Fry, 16, 1910, pp. 207-19 and 275-80.

238 Reed, *A Roger Fry Reader* (n. 38), p. 124.

239 R. Fry, 'The French Post-Impressionists', *Vision and Design*, London 1981, pp. 168-69.

240 Fry, 'Introduction', in *Animals in Chinese Art* (n. 163), p. 3.

Although Roger Fry's opinion that English art lacked honesty and clear thinking was criticized as a 'considerable bias', it was the architectural standards set by the Italian Renaissance that he sought.[241] After attempting to study old masters 'in the same spirit' as he might study contemporary artists, Fry encountered the same 'constructive design' in post-impressionism as in Chinese art.[242] He informed Goldsworthy Dickinson, 'I want to find out what the function of content is [...] all the essential aesthetic quality has to do with pure form.'[243] The 'purely esthetic enjoyment' offered by Chinese art as well as its 'leisured contemplation' was present in classical European art; as a result, the Chinese artist speaks to us 'in our own language' which has long been lost by 'our own ancestors', further suggesting that it would be extremely fruitful for 'our art' to not merely 'copy the form' but to absorb some of the spirit of Chinese art.[244] In his 1920s lectures, Fry argued that a completely representative Western painting is incomprehensible to the Chinese artist, who conveys reality in the 'creative language', expressing 'some of the profoundest conception of human spirit'.[245] A direct outcome of 'aesthetic impulses aiming at pure spiritual satisfactions', Chinese art is classic and free.[246]

The classic spirit played a prominent role in Roger Fry's Chinese art collection. The gilt-bronze garment plaque illustrating a pair of symmetrical creatures (Fig. 27) shows 'how the idea of animal life' penetrated the artist's imagination and how 'they could endow the simplest abstractions with life', while the bronze plaque (Fig. 28) of a 'feeble little newborn creature' was an example of the genius of abstracted life form.[247] The

241 R. Fry, 'Reflections on British Painting', in *French, Flemish and British Art*, London 1951, pp. 137-212; Spalding, *Roger Fry: Art and Life* (n. 19), p. 257.

242 Fry, 'Retrospect' (n. 88), pp. 201-2.

243 Fry, *Letters of Roger Fry* (n. 45), vol. I, p. 362.

244 Fry, 'Some Aspects of Chinese Art' (n. 150), p. 79.

245 Fry, 'Drawing or Design' (n. 108).

246 R. Fry, 'Scythian and Chinese', *The Arts of Painting and Sculpture*, London 1932, p. 79.

Fig. 27 – *Gilt-Bronze Garment Plaque*, 600 – 500 BC, China (Northern Hebei), H. 2.7 cm, W. 2.7 cm (The Courtauld Gallery, London). Illustrated in R. Fry, *Last Lectures*, Cambridge, 1939, Pl. 28, as *Scythian Brooch.*

Fig. 28 – *Bronze Pectoral Ornament in the Form of a Crouching Animal*, 600 – 500 BC, China (Northern Hebei), L. 4.5 cm (The Courtauld Gallery, London). Illustrated in R. Fry, *Last Lectures*, Cambridge, 1939, Pl. 29, as *Scythian Ornament*.

fact that the coiled animal motif had been found as early as the Hongshan (third millennium BC) culture and that the feline shape had Daoist religious connotations was of minor significance for Fry, who appreciated these objects for their effective portrayal of the 'inner nature of the beasts'.[248] An intense understanding of life and interpretation of movement allowed Chinese artists to suggest life by 'very slight deflections from an abstractly conceived scheme of form'.[249] These objects did not intend to describe nature, producing instead a realism that is fundamental and emitted from within, rather than imposed by imagination or imitation. It is a classic spirit interpretable through geometrical forms and the vividness of animal life. The same is true of the Guanyin (Fig. 29), Fry's 'biggest' purchase of Chinese art.[250] Brought out of China by Paul Pelliot and exhibited at the Burlington Fine Arts Club, it was acquired by Fry in 1913 from Charles Vignier's gallery in Paris before being sold in 1925 'owing to hard times'.[251] Fry was so fond of the sculpture that he had a plaster cast made before parting with it.[252] Considered by Fry as 'the finest example in this country of this particular style', its oval forms coupled with rhythmic flow of drapery lines perfectly exemplify the 'instinctive feeling for the animating spirit' that Fry thought 'the East nearly always felt'.[253] Buddhist imagery was assimilated and translated by Chinese sculptors into their own 'plastic idioms' as they created expressive forms not only 'of an idealized humanity' but also 'of the serenity attained by pure

---

247 Illustrated in Fry, Last Lectures (n. 104), as pls. 28, *Scythian Brooch*, and 29, as *Scythian Ornament*, respectively; Fry, *Last Lectures* (n. 104), p. 128.

248 E. Bunker, *Ancient Bronzes of the Eastern Eurasian Steppes from the Arthur M. Sackler Collection*, New York 1997, pp. 188, 194; Fry, *Last Lectures* (n. 104), p. 128.

249 Fry, 'Chinese Bronzes at Messrs. Yamanaka's' (n. 7).

250 C. Green, 'Roger Fry's Canon', in *Art Made Modern*, ed. C. Green, London 2000, p. 150.

251 Fry, *Letters of Roger Fry* (n. 45), vol. I, p. 54; Burlington Fine Arts Club, *Catalogue of a Collection of Objects of Chinese Art*, London 1915, p. 25; Green, 'Roger Fry's Canon' (n. 250), p. 150; R. Fry, unpublished letter to Raymond Henniker-Heaton, object archive 1925. 118, 1925, Worcester Art Museum, MA.

252 L. Virgin and S. Abe, communication, 2010 – 2011, Worcester Art Museum, MA.

253 Ibid.; Fry, *Last Lectures* (n. 104), p. 133.

contemplation and detachment from the world of illusion'.[254] Noticing the same tenderness of expression in a pair of Wei dancing statuettes (Fig. 30) in his collection, Fry compared them to thirteenth-century French sculptures of similar predominant mood.[255] Despite wrongly identifying the modern copies as authentic, he declared that the expressive power of Wei sculptures lay in expression of complex mood and character through simplicity of form.[256] As the 'Tragic spirit' exhibited in Western art was unknown to the Chinese, their 'most exalted religious feeling' led them to a 'more contemplative mood' remote from immediate action.[257]

For Arthur Waley, the classic spirit emanated from Chinese art theories. Xie He's fifth-century 'Liu Fa' ('Six Principles') was the first systematic theoretical approach to Chinese painting. With an earlier translation by Herbert Giles described as 'extra-terse', the question of the Chinese punctuation of Xie's principles was not resolved until Qian Zhongshu's suggestion in 1979, interpreting it similarly to the way Waley had done over half a century earlier.[258] Waley translated the sixth principle *chuan yi mo xie* as 'by handing on and copying to transmit designs', considering this 'particularly Chinese' art to 'echo' the past and be 'classical'.[259] He failed to notice, however, that this method could also imply that the artist should edit and perfect his sketch before transmitting the pattern to a formal picture, leading him to understand the classic spirit in

---

254 Fry, 'Scythian and Chinese' (n. 246), p. 71.

255 Illustrated in Fry, *Last Lectures* (n. 104), pl. 225, as *Wei Statuettes*; Fry, *Last Lectures* (n. 104), p. 141.

256 As rediscovered by Professor Jean Michel Massing, King's College, University of Cambridge.

257 Fry, 'Some Aspects of Chinese Art' (n. 150), pp. 79-80.

258 J. Ferguson, *Outlines of Chinese Art*, Chicago, 1919, pp. 206-7; Z. Li, 'Taolun Qian Zhongshu "Liufa" Shidu Shuo' ('Discussion on Qian Zhongshu's "Six Principles" and Lost Meanings'), *Xueshu Jiaoliu (Academic Exchange)*, 4 (109), 2003. For detail see Z. Qian, *Guan Zhui Bian (Limited Views: Essays on Ideas and Letters)*, Beijing 1979.

259 A. Waley, 'Chinese Philosophy of Art – I. Note on the "Six Methods"', *The Burlington Magazine for Connoisseurs*, 37, 1920, pp. 309-10 (309).

Fig. 29 – *Guanyin*, Sui dynasty (590 – 618), stone, H. 88.9 cm (Worchester Art Museum, MA).

Fig. 30 – *A Pair of Figures*, 20th century, ceramic (The Fitzwilliam Museum, Cambridge). Illustrated in R. Fry, *Last Lectures*, Cambridge, 1939, Pl. 225, as *Wei Statuettes*.

Chinese art as associated solely with past designs.[260] Explaining the first principle *qi yun sheng dong* (spirit-harmony – life's motion), Waley stressed the spirit's status as 'objective' and 'outside the artist', and argued that it was the painter's task to illustrate the 'operations of the spirit' producing 'Life's Motion', an interpretation relied upon decades later by Alexander Soper when discussing Chinese figural paintings.[261] For Waley, this principle was essential; without it, Xie was at most a 'colour-photographer' whose major aim was to imitate and record.[262]

Analysing Wang Wei's rejection of direct imitation of nature, Arthur Waley stated that landscape painting 'perfects nature and completes the Creator's work', not only showing the artist's adherence to Zen Buddhism but also forming the basis of many European art theories.[263] Although Waley did not elaborate further, his view was similar to Roger Fry's, who believed that art was not just a reflection of the perceived world but generated 'the conviction of a new and definite reality'.[264] Wang's monochrome painting, inspired by the Buddhist belief that one should turn away from the 'outward show' or *rūpa* of the world, was classical as it embodied the same 'emotion caused by reading a poem', an analysis shared by Wang Shixiang, who considered Wang's poems and paintings as merely different forms of the same *nei xing* (inner character).[265] That Wang is the ancestor of subsequent landscape painters whose pictures are 'undeniably poetical' is vital;

---

260 'Introduction', *The Tradition of Re-Presenting in Art: Originality and Reproduction in Chinese Painting and Calligraphy*, National Palace Museum (website) 2008.

261 Waley, 'Chinese Philosophy of Art – I. Note on the "Six Methods"' (n. 259); A. Soper, 'Life-Motion and the Sense of Space in Early Chinese Representational Art', *The Art Bulletin*, 30 (3), 1948, pp. 167-86.

262 Waley, 'Chinese Philosophy of Art – I. Note on the "Six Methods"' (n. 259).

263 A. Waley, 'Chinese Philosophy of Art – II. Wang Wei and Chang Yen-Yüan', *The Burlington Magazine for Connoisseurs*, 38, 1921, p. 32.

264 Fry, 'The French Post-Impressionists' (n. 239), p. 167.

265 The Sanskrit term *rūpa*, translated into Chinese, is se (colour). See Waley, *An Introduction* (n. 116), pp. 144-45; S. Wang, *Zhongguo Hualun Yanjiu (Study on Chinese Painting Theory)*, vol. I, Beijing 2014, p. 49.

further, the passion for nature in which Buddha is omnipresent suits the expression of literature better than painting.[266] In likening Wang's painting to poetry, Waley emphasized the expression of inner spirit through a visual medium, rather than the mere imitation of appearance. For Waley, the classical spirit embodies a poetical emotion bestowed by nature and passed down from one's ancestors; it is a setting into motion of life's forces, transmitted through the 'breaking up' or 'disarraying' of ink washes in a ritual performance.[267] The poetical element of the classic spirit was also noted by Fry, who emphasized the 'unity of a picture' was preconditioned by its 'perfect conformity to a poetical idea' and the subordination of its parts to 'a single easily-apprehended pattern'.[268] It is the poetical ideal that unifies the formal aspects of painting: as 'poetry becomes more intense the content is entirely remade by the form' and 'the sense of poetry is analogous to the things represented in painting'.[269] It was a particular relation of form to content that Fry saw in the classical spirit of poetry and painting.

Arthur Waley's almost obstinate respect for the classic spirit of Chinese art led him to conclude that the Mongols of the Yuan (1271 – 1368) dynasty had no impact on 'the development of Chinese civilisation'. For him, Yuan culture was written 'entirely by and for Chinese' for whom the 'archaistic revival' of the Tang dynasty was seen as most appropriate.[270] The homage paid to tradition was regarded as a 'creative' and 'revolutionary' 'originality' by later scholars such as Sherman Lee, with Ni Zan's legendary 'purity' and 'loftiness' creating a classic sense of desolation, imitated and copied by both his contemporaries and future artists.[271] Wen Fong not only considered the revival of Northern Song landscape idioms in Yuan an innovation, but the

266 Waley, An Introduction (n. 116), pp. 144-45; A. Waley, *Zen Buddhism and Its Relation to Art,* London 1922, p. 24.

267 Waley, *An Introduction* (n. 116), pp. 146-47.

268 Fry, 'Introduction' (n. 91), in *Discourses,* p. XVIII.

269 Fry, *Letters of Roger Fry* (n. 45), vol. I, p. 362.

270 Waley, *An Introduction* (n. 116), p. 237.

271 S. Lee, *Chinese Landscape Painting*, Cleveland 1962, pp. 39 and 47.

'calligraphic landscape art' of Zhao Mengfu as an exponent of 'the scholar-painter's aesthetic'.[272] In his subtle criticism ofZhao's conservatism, Waley failed to inspect Zhao's calligraphy, which fascinated the Chinese more than his painting, and which could have instigated his discovery of the classic spirit in Zhao's works.[273] Waley's insistence on the 'Chineseness' of Yuan is likely due to his preference for Tang pictures, which more closely embody the classical spirit and were considered the 'golden age of painting' by Roger Fry.[274]

For Goldsworthy Dickinson, the Chinese spirit was expressed via rationalism, scepticism and Confucianism's stress on conduct.[275] Whilst incorporating the classical spirit of Chinese art, Confucianism was not to be understood as a religion but rather as a fundamental creed for life, a view which had already been expressed by Han Yü who considered it more a way of life than an academic discipline.[276] Ancestor worship, a primary principle of Confucianism, considers all past and future lives as a unity and, Dickinson claimed, finds its Western counterpart in Roman civilization.[277] The continuity and unity of time and space through institutional structure is the source of the classical spirit. Dickinson's pioneering analysis of Confucianism and its impact on art history was unique, particularly at a time when most Western scholars studied Chinese art through the narrow lenses of Daoism and Buddhism, considering Confucianism only in terms of its political and social effects.[278] Although often misinterpreted from angles of moral and ceremonial pedantry, Confucius was a man of aesthetic perception, mindful of art's nature and function in society.[279] While later art historians such

272 W. Fong, *Summer Mountains: The Timeless Landscape*, New York 1975.

273 Lee, *Chinese Landscape Painting* (n. 271), p. 40.

274 Fry, *Last Lectures* (n. 104), p. 144.

275 Dickinson, 'An Essay on the Civilisations of India, China and Japan' (n. 8), p. 65.

276 Dickinson, 'Letters from John Chinaman' (n. 6), pp. 32-3; W. de Bary, 'A Reappraisal of Neo-Confucianism', in *Studies in Chinese Thought*, ed. A. Wright, Chicago 1953, p. 85.

277 Dickinson, 'Letters from John Chinaman' (n. 6), pp. 32-3.

278 De Bary, 'A Reappraisal of Neo-Confucianism' (n. 276), p. 81.

279 W. Speiser, *China Spirit and Society*, London 1960, pp. 18-20.

as Osvald Sirén, Victoria Contag and Laurence Sickman would expand upon this notion, it would not be until James Cahill's examination of Confucianism's impact on painting theory that its elements were given due credit in Chinese art by Western scholars.[280]

Sometimes described as a 'Socratic inquirer' with an ardent interest in classics, Goldsworthy Dickinson argued that the classical spirit of Chinese art and civilization mirrors the Greek spirit, the evocation of which in our modern age could salvage mankind, as progress should be conceived of in societal rather than individual terms.[281] Dickinson believed that just as China served as a reference point from which other Asian countries 'took their ideas', ancient Greece served a similar function in shaping modern Western life.[282] This view was shared by Bertrand Russell, who found in China 'most of what was to be found in Greece'.[283] Dickinson's writings on ancient Greece and its art shed light on the classical spirit of Chinese ideology, mirroring the Confucian belief that nobility in painting reflects the virtue of the artist. Although Roger Fry and Arthur Waley saw the equal treatment of all life forms in Chinese art as antagonistic to Greek philosophy, Dickinson considered the primary care for mankind as prevalent in the incarnation of the classic spirit.[284] This dichotomy was further expanded upon by John Ferguson who contrasted anthropocentric Greek art with its Chinese counterpart in which man was a small part of the creation. This,

---

280 J. Cahill, 'Confucian Elements in the Theory of Painting', in *The Confucian Persuasion*, ed. A. Wright, Stanford 1960, p. 335.

281 'Obituary', The Times, August 4, 1932, The Papers of Goldsworthy Lowes Dickinson, King's College Archive, GLD/6/9; 'Obituary', *The Cambridge Review*, October 14, 1932, The Papers of Goldsworthy Lowes Dickinson, King's College Archive, GLD/6/9; G. Dickinson, 'The Contribution of Ancient Greece to Modern Life', *Letters from John Chinaman and Other Essays*, London 1946, p. 105; G. Dickinson, *Religion and Immortality*, London 1933, pp. 40-42.

282 Dickinson, 'An Essay on the Civilisations of India, China and Japan' (n. 8), p. 76; Dickinson, 'The Contribution of Ancient Greece to Modern Life' (n. 281), p. 88.

283 B. Russell, *The Problem of China*, London 1922, p. 192.

284 Ferguson, *Outlines of Chinese Art* (n. 258), pp. 208-10.

however, should not be considered an insurmountable discrepancy. Fry and Waley's emphasis was on the imposed human ideal of the depicted object, while Dickinson focused on the familiarization of supernatural and otherwise uninterpretable forces. According to Dickinson, the human being is considered one of the universe's elements in Chinese art.[285] This humble perception of mankind should be regarded as compatible with views of the other Trio members that animals and plants are of equal importance in Chinese art. A similar approach, resulting from the Confucian approach to objects, was described decades later by Victoria Contag, who noted that the size of human figures in relation to their landscape diminished in painting by 'educated' artists of later dynasties, representing their diminished significance as beings of the universe.[286] The major difference between Greek and Chinese art for Dickinson lay in their treatment of nature, with the former treating it as a mere 'background to human activity' while the latter appreciated it for its own sake, an attitude shared by the 'modern and romantic' movements in the West.[287]

The Modernity of Chinese Art

For Roger Fry, the modernity of Chinese art was already present in Han artists whose attitudes were similar to those of modern painters. Marked by psychological representation of individual characters (Fig. 17), the 'linear design' and energy indicated by 'slight suggestions of movement' was revived in Tang art, whose balanced design shows a 'highly deliberate and complete art'.[288] Simple linear design is used to convey emotions. Chinese landscape painting, aimed at spiritual satisfaction rather than representation, achieved this via watercolours on silk and through their handwritten nature.[289] Watercolourists could call attention to the untouched surfaces between different parts of the total

285 Dickinson, 'An Essay on the Civilisations of India, China and Japan' (n. 8), p. 66.

286 V. Contag, 'The Unique Characteristics of Chinese Landscape Pictures', *Archives of the Chinese Art Society of America*, 6, 1952, p. 59.

287 G. Dickinson, *The Greek View of Life*, New York 1911, pp. 204-5.

288 Fry, Last Lectures (n. 104), p. 144.

vision, suggesting various interpretations.[290] The atmosphere suggested by spaces and intervals on silk surfaces allowed for the play of imagination, while the calligraphic quality of brushwork conveyed the artist's sensibilities through rhythmic lines. This affective aspect of art was deemed sufficiently important by Robin Collingwood that he incorporated into his philosophical inquiries of aesthetics.[291] Marvelling at the variety of motives and modernity of approach represented by Tang and Song artists, Fry observed that expressionism in China could already be noticed in Muxi Fachang's landscapes of the thirteenth century (Fig. 31).[292] For Fry, the eighth-century fresco from Dunhuang (Fig. 32) has a 'strangely moving effect' achieved by 'odd perspective' and 'patterned treatment' of the subject, showing 'resourceful power' to convey spatial impressions as well as an 'extraordinary feeling for interval'.[293] Similarly, he argued that the Song imitation of Tang artist Wang Wei (Fig. 33) displays detachment from 'ordinary concerns of life', presenting a sophisticated response to 'natural appearances' achievable only through contemplation.[294] Analysing the aesthetics of 'Boating by Moonlight' (Fig. 34) by Song landscapist Ma Yuan, Fry commented that no parallel in European art existed before the nineteenth century.[295] The suggestion of scenery veiled by mist presents 'little plastic opportunity', brings the viewer into direct contact with the 'peculiar mood of melancholy reverie' through 'shapes' and 'tone washes' rather than formal design, and reveals a profound sensitivity to the 'mood of nature' provoked by

289 Fry, 'Scythian and Chinese' (n. 246), pp. 65-80.

290 Fry, 'Chinese Art and Architecture' (n. 148), p. 34.

291 R. Collingwood, *The Principles of Art*, London 1958, pp. 105-17.

292 Image from O. Sirén, *A History of Early Chinese Painting*, vol. II, London 1933, pl. 83. Fry, 'Review of *A History of Early Chinese Painting* by Osvald Sirén' (n. 126), p. 17.

293 Image from P. Pelliot, *Les grottes de Touen-Houang: peintures et sculptures bouddhiques des époques des Wei, des T'ang et des Song, tome second, grottes 31 à 72*, Paris 1920, pl. CXXIV. Illustrated in R. Fry, *Last Lectures* (104), pl. 244; also in Waley, *An Introduction* (n. 116), pl. XVII.

294 Illustrated in Fry, *Last Lectures* (n. 104), as Song imitation, pl. 247; Fry, *Last Lectures* (n. 104), pp. 148-49.

295 R. Fry, 'Characteristics of French Art', *French, Flemish and British Art*, London 1951, p. 32.

Fig. 31 – Muxi Fachang (1210 – 1269), *Returning Boats* (Count Matsudaira, Tokyo), and *A Fishing Village* (Collection of Nezu, Tokyo), image from O. Sirén, *A History of Early Chinese Painting*, vol. 2, London, 1933, Pl. 83.

Fig. 32 – *The Fight for Buddha's Relics*, ca. 700, wall painting from Dunhuang, cave 70, image from P. Pelliot, *Les grottes de Touen-Houang: peintures et sculptures bouddhiques des époques des Wei, des T'ang et des Song, tome second, grottes 31 à 72*, Paris, 1920, Pl. CXXIV. Illustrated in R. Fry, *Last Lectures*, Cambridge, 1939, Pl. 244; also in A. Waley, *An Introduction to the Study of Chinese Painting*, London, 1958 (First published 1923), Pl. XVII.

Fig. 33 – After Wang Wei, *Clearing After Snowfall Along the River*, mid-16th century, handscroll, ink and colour on paper, 29.2 x 446.0 cm (Honolulu Museum of Art, HI, formerly Luo Zhenyu collection). Illustrated in R. Fry, *Last Lectures*, as Song imitation, Cambridge, 1939, Pl. 247.

Fig. 34 –Attributed to Ma Yuan, *Boating by Moonlight*, Southern Song dynasty (1127 – 1279), hanging scroll, ink and colour on silk, 172.5 x 85.2 cm (The British Museum, London, formerly Eumorfopoulos collection).

'prolonged and dispassionate contemplation'.[296] For Fry the poetics of landscape painting lies in the emotion and atmosphere suggested by elements of design, leading Chinese painting from the Song period towards a 'romantic and expressionist attitude'.[297] According to Fry, the Chinese disregard of light and shade, coupled with sensitivity of subtle tone relations in expressing atmosphere, 'anticipated Western art by nearly 1,000 years'. 'Nothing quite like this can be seen in Europe before the later nineteenth century [...] Perhaps Seurat gives us our nearest European parallel and he, too, […] relied mainly for his expression upon the feeling for intervals.'[298]

Roger Fry defined modern art as 'the tradition which began with Giotto, and arose out of an art which lived for centuries as an obscure and parasite growth upon the decayed remains of the art of Greece and Rome'.[299] It was the 'rarest imaginative power' and the 'whole range of human emotions' expressed through simple, direct and literal lines that made Giotto a 'modern' painter.[300] In his 1910 article 'Oriental Art', published in *Quarterly Review*, Fry commented on the revelation of Asian art that would benefit European artists in their 'return to the essential principles which have been upheld more conscientiously in the East than in the West'.[301] Referring to French post-impressionists, but also to Paul Cézanne, whom he compared to masters such as Rembrandt van Rijn and Leonardo da Vinci, he assumed that comparable formal features were created in similar spirit.[302] Overwhelmed by

296 Fry, 'The Eumorfopoulos Collection' (n. 176), pp. 652-53; R. Fry, 'The Chinese Exhibition', *Nation*, 1910, pp. 593-94.

297 Fry, 'The Eumorfopoulos Collection' (n. 176), pp. 652-53.

298 Fry, *Last Lectures* (n. 104), p. 149.

299 R. Fry, 'I. Transition from Classical to Modern Art', The Papers of Roger Eliot Fry, King's College Archive, REF/1/65/1.

300 R. Fry, 'Giotto', *Vision and Design*, London 1981, pp. 92-123.

301 Laing, *Roger Fry: An Annotated Bibliography of the Published Writings* (n. 173), p. 153.

302 R. Shiff, 'Painting, Writing, Handwriting', in R. Fry, *Cézanne: A Study of His Development*, Chicago and London 1989, p. xxiii.

the 'emptiness' or 'horrible resemblance' of conventional art, Cézanne relied on plastic and structural designs to bring out the truth — similar to the way Chinese artists had done centuries earlier.[303] Later art historians such as Jean Dubosc likened Cézanne to the Qing artist Wang Yuanqi whose 'surprisingly modern attitude' was shown in the classical austere composition aimed at bringing out the inner essence of nature.[304] Despite the initial furore and criticism the post-impressionist shows curated by Fry garnered, they not only had 'all England talking about contemporary painting' but also drove the 'more alert' public to look at 'primitive, Oriental, and savage art', according to Clive Bell.[305] It would be Bell who made the concept of 'Significant Form', or the aesthetically moving relations of lines and colours, the essential quality in art and a principle of aesthetics.[306] Although Heinrich Wölfflin had explored the dynamics of artistic style through rigorous formal analysis of opposing principles, he focused primarily on Renaissance and Baroque art, and it would be Fry who championed formalism in modern art criticism.[307] The rhythmic design, spatial relation and new use of colour by Henri Matisse sought an equivalence, rather than a likeness, to nature, approaching 'the ideals of Chinese art'.[308] This comparison was acknowledged by Alfred Barr, who viewed the 'essential forms and relationships' of Matisse's drawings as similar to the 'philosopher-poet-painters of the T'ang and Sung'.[309] As exemplified by Wang Wei, 'one of the greatest interpreters of landscape', the perception of scenery reveals 'a sense of overtones of feeling in the presence of nature' which is 'the special discovery of a

303 R. Fry, 'Paul Cézanne', *Vision and Design*, London 1981, pp. 181-85.

304 J. Dubosc, 'A New Approach to Chinese Painting', *Oriental Art*, 3 (2), 1950, pp. 50-57.

305 R. Shone, *Bloomsbury Portraits: Vanessa Bell, Duncan Grant and Their Circle*, London 1976, pp. 59-61.

306 C. Bell, *Art*, Dublin 1961, pp. 9-46.

307 A. D'Allava, *Methods and Theories of Art History*, London 2005, p. 18; D. Summers, 'Heinrich Wölfflin's "Kunstgeschichtliche Grundbegriffe", 1915', *The Burlington Magazine*, 151 (1276), 2009, p. 479.

308 Fry, 'The French Post-Impressionists' (n. 239), p. 168.

309 A. Barr, Jr., *Matisse, His Art and His Public*, New York 1951, pp. 149 and 276.

modern man'.[310] The 'photographic realism' in Yuan drawings (Fig. 35) exhibits a choice of quantity and interval of aesthetic purpose, a quality understood perhaps most thoroughly by Edgar Degas.[311] It is precisely these same characteristics created by free, expressive and spontaneous attitudes that Fry saw in Chinese art, and which rendered it modern. Fry's rigid formalist method paved the way for others, including Clement Greenberg, who not only agreed that the excitement of modern painting lay in its pure preoccupation with formal qualities to the exclusion of implications, but extended the approach to abstract expressionism as a continuous development of art history.[312]

The modernity of Chinese art was noted by Raphael Petrucci in 1910, who believed that the deep compassion and love shown towards all manifestations of life, as well as the combination of intellectual and emotional aspects in both thought and art, were what made Chinese art modern.[313] This notion may have inspired Roger Fry, whose 1911 review of *La philosophie de la nature dans l'art d'Extrême-Orient* referenced and elaborated this opinion through formal analysis. For Fry, Chinese art's modernity is also revealed by the simplicity, elegance and refinement of Song ceramics. Expressing emotions through control and adherence to rules, 'primitive' pottery is 'the purely plastic quality, the evidence of the most perfect control over matter, the impress of will without let or hindrance'.[314] Applying the term 'primitive' frequently to a variety of art across borders and ages, Fry was fascinated by rudimentary forms such as the tripod incense burner (Fig. 36) in his collection, which had been catalogued as Song due to its glaze

---

310 Fry, 'Review of *A History of Early Chinese Painting* by Osvald Sirén' (n. 126), p. 17.

311 Image from O. Sirén, *A History of Early Chinese Painting*, vol. II, London 1933, pl. 106. Illustrated in Fry, *Last Lectures* (n. 104), pl. 246; Fry, *Last Lectures* (n. 104), p. 148.

312 C. Green, 'Into the Twentieth Century: Roger Fry's Project Seen from 2000', in *Art Made Modern: Roger Fry's Vision of Art*, ed. C. Green, London 2000, pp. 13-14; C. Greenberg, 'Avant-Garde and Kitsch', *Art and Culture: Critical Essays*, Boston 1967, p. 7.

313 R. Fry, 'Review of *La philosophie de la nature dans l'art d'Extrême-Orient* by Raphael Petrucci', *The Burlington Magazine for Connoisseurs*, 19, 1911, pp. 106-107.

314 Fry, 'The Chinese Exhibition' (n. 296), pp. 593-94.

Fig. 35 – Zhao Mengfu (1254 – 1322), *Two Horses*, 38.7 x 64.1 cm (Collection of Adolphe Stoclet, Brussels), image from O. Sirén, *A History of Early Chinese Painting*, vol. 2, London, 1933, Pl. 106. Illustrated in R. Fry, *Last Lectures*, Cambridge, 1939, Pl. 246.

Fig. 36 – *Tripod Incense Burner*, Yuan dynasty (1279 – 1368), earthenware, H. 9.1 cm, D. 8.5 cm (The Courtauld Gallery, London).

which followed the Jun-ware tradition, despite its thick body and iron permeating redness suggesting an early Yuan dating.[315] For Fry, Chinese artists cultivated their 'sensual aptitudes' so that the 'material quality' of substance could be apprehended with a 'peculiar emotional exaltation', as was also evident in jades cut in forms of 'extreme simplicity' to accentuate the 'material quality' of the precious mineral.[316] Although Fry suggested that perfection of 'material quality' is aimed at by all artists 'more or less consciously', he argued that the Chinese were 'supreme' as seen in the 'simple undecorated pottery of the Sung period'.[317] The sensual connection between viewer and artwork was echoed by Henri Focillon, for whom matter's physical qualities such as 'weight, density, light, and colour' were indispensable to the transformation and continuity of form, and a Tang ceramic flask could equally have been 'a marvellous conglomerate created by subterranean fire or accident'.[318] According to Fry, the 'lyrical ecstasy' that the 'purely sensuous quality' of material provoked is a 'distinctive characteristic' the Chinese retained and developed.[319] This material quality was recognized by Rosalind Krauss when deciphering signs in Pablo Picasso's collages, whose 'material presence' and physical shape rather than representation achieved the visual 'metalanguage' and mark the threshold of postmodernist art.[320] Shape must have also attracted Fry to his incense burner as he discussed a Neolithic ware (Fig. 37) and Zhou bronze (Fig. 38) of similar shape in his lectures.[321] Its archaic

---

315 J. Stair, 'The Employment of Matter: Pottery of the Omega Workshop', in *Beyond Bloomsbury: Designs of the Omega Workshops 1913 – 19*, ed. A. Gerstein, London 2009, p. 28; for detail of the burner, see The Home House Trustees, *Catalogue of the Pictures and other Works of Art at Home House* (n. 48), p. 74, lot 125.

316 Fry, *Last Lectures* (n. 104), p. 109.

317 R. Fry, 'Review of *Chinese Porcelain and Hard Stones* by E. Gorer and J. F. Blacker', The Papers of Roger Eliot Fry, King's College Archive, REF/1/19.

318 H. Focillon, *The Life of Forms in Art*, New York 1948, pp. 31-41.

319 Fry, *Last Lectures* (n. 104), p. 109.

320 R. Krauss, 'In the Name of Picasso', *The Originality of the Avant-Garde and Other Modernist Myths*, London 1985, pp. 37-38; R. Krauss, *The Picasso Papers*, Cambridge, MA 1999, p. 28.

321 Images from Fry, *Last Lectures* (n. 104), pl. 139 and 140.

form, he argued, conveys a plastic feeling representative of a casual and primitive state of mind. An object for 'common life', it belongs to the category that inspired Fry to create the Omega workshop in 1913, a practical outlet of his modernist vision.[322] Despite the 'impeccable taste' of the imperial factory in Ming and Qing periods, the lack of elegance and plastic feeling in later ceramics propelled Fry to concentrate on earlier wares, a preference that explains why half of his Chinese ceramics collection came from the Song period.[323]

Revealing the reality of life without pretence is a modern aspect of Chinese art acknowledged by Arthur Waley, for whom the poetry of Bai Jüyi was the epitome, echoing Goldsworthy Dickinson's observation that Chinese art was 'realism' showing 'a vision of what this life is as seen by those who can see it'.[324] Marvelling at the 'immense originality' of the poet, who 'almost alone of T'ang poets, avoided the pedantry of obscure literary allusion', he applauded the 'self-revelation' and care for 'human life' of Bai's style that had 'never existed in China' before. Waley's appreciation of Bai was so strong that sixty out of *A Hundred and Seventy Chinese Poems* published in 1918 were from Bai's oeuvre.[326] Appropriating literature into visual art, the humanistic and empathetic emotion vital for modernity is embedded in the Buddhist tradition of Chinese art, especially Zen Buddhism. This

322 Stair, 'The Employment of Matter: Pottery of the Omega Workshop' (n. 315), p. 28.

323 R. Fry, 'Richard Bennet Collection of Chinese Porcelain', *The Burlington Magazine for Connoisseurs*, 1911, p. 137; Roger Fry may have been influenced by Arthur Waley's translation of Gao Lian's *Zun Sheng Ba Jian (Eight Treatises on Guarding Life)* in which Gao's view on Song wares was expressed. For detail see 'The Tsun Sheng Pa Chien, A.D. 1591 by Kao Lien', in *The Year Book of Oriental Art and Culture 1924 – 1925*, transl. and ed. A. Waley, London 1925, pp. 80-87. Later, art historian Ernst Gombrich studied the phenomenon that older less sophisticated 'primitive' art is often considered superior to later more refined art in the Western tradition. See E. H. Gombrich, *The Preference for the Primitive: Episodes in the History of Western Taste and Art*, London 2002.

324 Dickinson, 'An Essay on the Civilisations of India, China and Japan' (n. 8), p. 66.

325 A. Waley, 'Further Poems by Po Chu-I', The Papers of Arthur David Waley, King's College Archive, ADW/4/2, undated (after 1918); Waley, *An Introduction* (n. 116), pp. 102-103.

326 'He Never Went to China – A Portrait of Arthur Waley' (n. 9), p. 139.

Fig. 37 – *Tripod Pot*, Yangshao culture (5000 – 3000 BC) (Östasiatiska Museet, Stockholm), image from R. Fry, *Last Lectures*, Cambridge, 1939, Pl. 139.

Fig. 38 – *Bronze Tripod*, Zhou dynasty (1046 – 256 BC) (Calmann collection, Paris), image from R. Fry, *Last Lectures*, Cambridge, 1939, Pl. 140.

'sect' often occurred in books on the Far East as a 'school of abstract meditation' that exerted 'a profound influence upon art and literature', though little about Zen and the 'exact nature' of its impact on art had been said, according to Waley.[327]

Arthur Waley's 1922 *Zen Buddhism and Its Relation to Art* was one of the earliest studies on the topic published in Europe, stirring a passion in the author that would last until the day of his death, on which he was making notes on the Southern Zen School.[328] This religious aspect of Chinese culture was deemed so pivotal to the understanding of Chinese painting that he incorporated this publication into *An Introduction to the Study of Chinese Painting*, with additional chapters dedicated to Zen painters. For Waley, Zen Buddhism is indispensable to the understanding of Chinese art history, as art was regarded as 'a kind of Zen' through which time is obliterated and the universe is viewed 'in its primal unity'; it is 'in the language of Zen' that art is discussed in China and Japan after the twelfth century.[329] James Cahill criticized Waley as 'incautious' for having made such a statement without being sufficiently acquainted with Song and later Chinese art literature, as well as for relying too much on Japanese art historical scholarship while neglecting other streams of thought.[330] Ernest Fenollosa, for instance, whose works Waley consulted, argued that Northern Song experienced an almost complete transition to Zen Buddhism, joining hands with Daoism as an opposition to Confucian teachings.[331] For Waley, Zen Buddhism was the emotional condition of the creator: by understanding this, the viewer could achieve an empathetic connection with the artist. Zen annihilates the consciousness so that art is produced by 'an interaction of conscious and unconscious faculties'. The shared

---

327 Waley, *Zen Buddhism and Its Relation to Art* (n. 266), p. 7.

328 F. Johns, 'Bibliography: Introducing the East', 1968, The Papers of Arthur David Waley, King's College Archive, ADW/4/5.

329 Waley, *Zen Buddhism and Its Relation to Art* (n. 266), p. 22.

330 Cahill, 'Confucian Elements in the Theory of Painting' (n. 280), pp. 115-16.

331 E. Fenollosa, *Epochs of Chinese and Japanese Art*, vol. II, London 1912, pp. 1-2.

understanding between artist and public about the conditions under which art is created was more important than a 'sound aesthetic'.[332] The Zen artist does not aim to achieve beauty, but rather an identification with the depicted object and the externalization of its inner Buddha. The omnipresence of Buddha, as well as all things that exist, either 'animate or inanimate', are 'utterances of the Absolute'.[333]

Although the co-existence of Daoism and Confucianism contributed to Chinese art, Arthur Waley's overemphasis on Zen should be understood as the result of a high regard for the relation between art and emotion, a concept vital for Roger Fry's modern aesthetics.[334] In agreeing with Jin Hao's position that 'art consists of something more than mere representation' and that resemblance is not pictorial 'Truth', as well as criticizing Guo Xi's account that landscape painting should be representative and reminiscent of familiar places, Waley agreed with Fry that art should not be a mere representation of nature but should also convey empathetic emotions.[335] While for Fry the modernity of Chinese art is exhibited in formal features, Waley's modernity is achieved by absorbing Zen Buddhism into the creative process. The inner life of animals shown in Chinese art (Fig. 13) is equivalent to the life of the Zen artist, both of which are 'utterances' of Buddha. Through methods of self-hypothesis and indulgence in nature, the difference between the two lives is extinguished as man's universal consciousness brings the two into one. Furthermore, according to Waley, the 'Zen picture' belongs to the art of calligraphy rather than to painting, as exemplified by the tenth-century Zen artist Shi Ke, renowned for his eccentric characters as well as calligraphic strokes (Fig. 39).[336] The

332 Waley, *Zen Buddhism and Its Relation to Art* (n. 266), p. 22.

333 Waley, *An Introduction* (n. 116), p. 230.

334 Lee, *Chinese Landscape Painting* (n. 271), pp. 5-7.

335 A. Waley, 'Chinese Philosophy of Art – III. Ching Hao', *The Burlington Magazine for Connoisseurs*, 38 (216), 1921, pp. 111-12; Waley, 'Chinese Philosophy of Art – IV. Kuo His (Part I)' (n. 119), pp. 244-47.

336 Waley, *Zen Buddhism and Its Relation to Art* (n. 266), p. 24; Waley, *An Introduction* (n. 116), pp. 227-30.

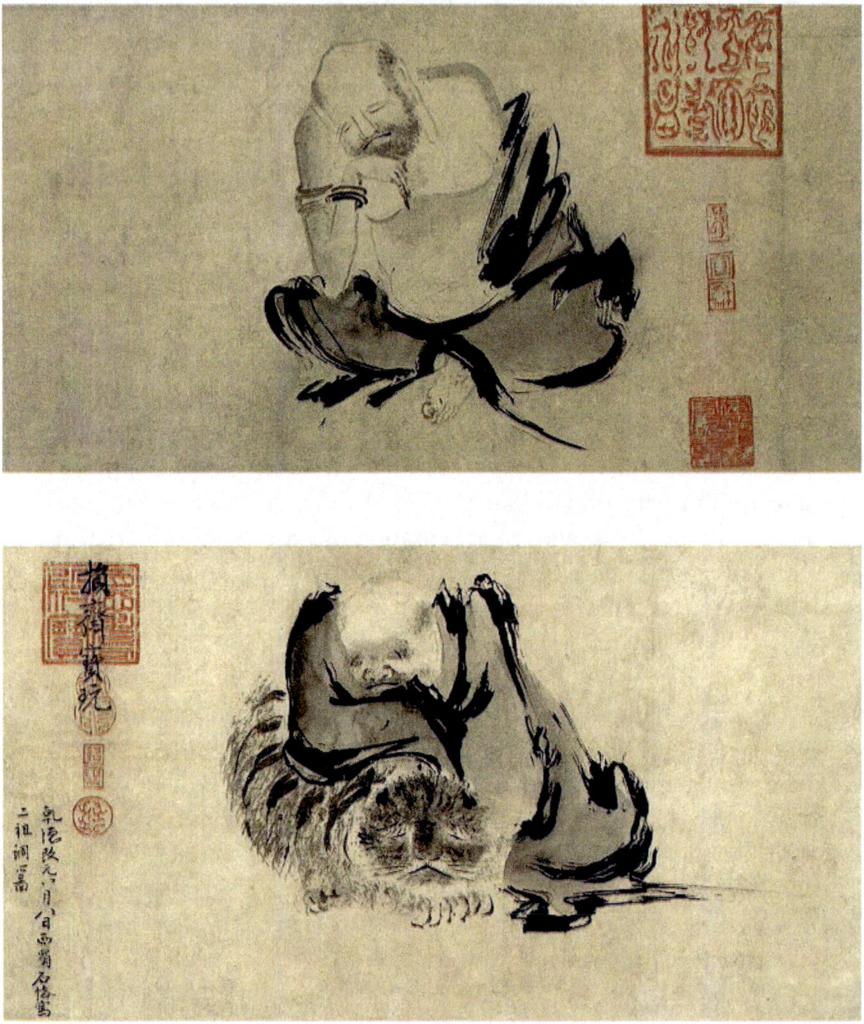

Fig. 39 – After Shi Ke, *The Second Patriarch in Contemplation*, 13th century, two hanging scrolls, ink on paper, 35.3 x 64.4 cm (Tokyo National Museum, Tokyo).

pontaneity of Shi's brushwork was also noticed by James Cahill, who considered it suitable for the needs of Zen, while anticipating future Zen paintings that depended primarily on the developmental transformations of the 'untrammeled' style.[337] Muxi Fachang meanwhile not only inherited the 'swift' and 'erratic' monochrome of Shi but also 'congealed' this passion into 'a stupendous calm' (Fig. 40).[338] Acknowledging that historical information about Muxi had only became available to Westerners after Waley published *Zen Buddhism and its Relation to Art*, Osvald Sirén suggested that the influence of 'the greatest genius' Muxi had so far been underestimated in China.[339] Largely due to Waley's effort, Muxi is today recognized by both domestic and foreign scholars as one of China's most important artists. It would be Julian Bell, also a member of King's College, who developed the calmness of Muxi's depictions of fruit into an account of the painter's sense of self and individuality.[340] Shi's strokes, typically dashed out in a drunken frenzy, represented life's motion in a controlled manner, whereas Muxi's motionless fruit is a concentration of life's energy where the absolute resides; although different in style they are both manifestations of Zen. This calligraphic spirit was observed by Fry, who appreciated the linear rhythm of handwriting which records the 'unconscious reaction' and the 'most direct expressions' of the artist.[341] Fry recognized the 'significance of brush work' in landscape that bestows 'a mode of literary feeling' onto a painting as 'plastic aims' become secondary. While the appreciation of Chinese painting via brushwork forms was pioneered by Zhao Mengfu and further elaborated by Wang Yuanqi, a theory of 'brushwork behaviour' was eventually established by Joan Stanley-Baker after

---

337 J. Cahill, *Chinese Painting*, Cleveland 1960, pp. 47-49.

338 Illustrated in Waley, *An Introduction* (n. 116), pl. XLIV. Waley, An Introduction (n. 116), pp. 230-31.

339 Sirén, *A History of Early Chinese Painting* (n. 292), vol. II, p. 93.

340 J. Bell, *What is Painting? Representation and Modern Art*, Hong Kong 1999, p. 136.

341 Fry, 'Chinese Art and Architecture' (n. 148), p. 35.

342 J. Kuo, Yishu Shi yu *Yishu Piping (Art History and Criticism)*, Taipei 2007, pp. 223-24 and 240-68.

Fig. 40 – Muxi Fachang (1210 – 1269), *Six Persimmons*, album leaf, ink on paper, 35.9 x 28.6 cm (Daitoku-ji, Kyoto). Illustrated in A. Waley, *An Introduction to the Study of Chinese Painting*, London, 1958 (First published 1923), Pl. XLIV.

interviewing Wang Jiqian in the 1970s.[343] The superficial contrast between the 'sentimental exaggeration' (Fig. 31) noted by Fry and calm serenity (Fig. 40) mentioned by Waley is effortlessly merged in Zen Buddhism.[344] Although Waley did not fully consider Daoism and Confucianism's relation to art, his translations and interpretations of philosophical texts such as *Dao De Jing (The Way and Its Power)* and *Lun Yü (The Analects of Confucius)* were used by subsequent scholars. As Michael Sullivan wrote, Waley's observation that the negative, passive and female element alone had access to *Dao* could be helpful for understanding the 'mystical sexual element' in Six Dynasties (220 – 589) landscape painting. Furthermore, Waley's interpretation of Zhuangzi's *wu wei* (nonaction) as a 'lyrical, almost ecstatic' attitude furthered the understanding of Chinese landscape painting as a proclamation of nature's harmony and man's ridiculous efforts to alter destiny.[345]

According to Goldsworthy Dickinson, Chinese art and poetry embodied the 'spirit of Wordsworth' and the most modern French literary movement.[346] The Chinese attitude towards life is and 'always has been' that of 'the most modern West'. Dickinson described the literati in China, 'a class of men' set to the 'pursuit of liberal arts' and 'functions of government', which have existed 'for many centuries past'.[347] Although Arthur Waley criticized 'Learned Man's Painting' for its rigid imitation of antique style in 'a complicated ritual' as well as sentimentality or 'facile emotionalism' of 'popular appeal', Dickinson believed that the lack of 'hereditary caste' made Chinese society 'the most democratic in the world', allowing people of all classes to respect things of the mind and spirit.[348] The social mobility inherent in the literati and officialdom ensured that their art could appreciate the 'most simple and universal relations of life', could feel and

---

343 J. Stanley-Baker, *Hua Yu Lu (Dialogue on Painting)*, transl. M. Wang, Guiling 2014.

344 Fry, 'Review of *A History of Early Chinese Painting* by Osvald Sirén' (n. 126), p. 17.

345 M. Sullivan, 'Pictorial Art and the Attitude Toward Nature in Ancient China', *The Art Bulletin*, 36 (1), 1954, pp. 5-6.

346 Dickinson, 'An Essay on the Civilisations of India, China and Japan' (n. 8), pp. 66-67.

347 Dickinson, 'Letters from John Chinaman' (n. 6), p. 27.

understand nature, as well as express the poignancy and sensitivity of mankind.[349] For Dickinson, it is the connection to nature and the externalization of human emotion and spirit embedded in the non-hierarchical structure of Chinese society that renders its art modern. Just as Roger Fry traced its origin to the antique past, modernity for Dickinson did not consist in creating new things but in disseminating the continued poetic perception of nature from past lives. He believed that the Chinese only had to discard their superstition, namely 'the discrediting of Confucianism', to be 'immediately in line with the West'. The discrepancies between the two were superficial and easily bridgeable as the Chinese were the 'most educable of people', inherently receptive to Western ideas.[350] This comparative approach influenced future research, such as Eileen Power's formation of colonialist feminist theories.[351] Failing to mention the hereditary nature of feudal lords and official titles, Dickinson's idealization has sometimes been interpreted as the 'instrumental needs' for his 'anti-Western polemic', leading to his unambiguous glorification of Chinese civilization and art.[352] However, rather than taking his statements literally, his efforts should be understood as constituting the search for an alternative for the West in which the 'renewal of art' must take place, a trend Fry believed had begun with the post-impressionists, who interrogated truth in a manner similar to the Chinese a millennium earlier.[353]

---

348 A. Waley, 'Chinese Philosophy of Art – VI', *The Burlington Magazine for Connoisseurs*, 39 (221), 1921, pp. 84 and 89; A. Waley, 'Chinese Philosophy of Art – VII. Tung Ch'i-ch'ang (1)', *The Burlington Magazine for Connoisseurs*, 39 (222), 1921, pp. 129-30; A. Waley, 'Ricci and Tung Ch'i-Ch'ang', *Bulletin of the School of Oriental and African Studies*, 2 (2), 1922, pp. 342-43; Waley, *An Introduction* (n. 116), p. 148.

349 Dickinson, 'Letters from John Chinaman' (n. 6), p. 27.

350 Dickinson, 'An Essay on the Civilisations of India, China and Japan' (n. 8), p. 65.

351 B. Melman, 'Under the Western Historian's Eyes: Eileen Power and the Early Feminist Encounter with

Colonialism', *History Workshop Journal*, 42, 1996, p. 155.

352 Harding, 'Goldsworthy Lowes Dickinson' (n. 12), p. 30.

353 Dickinson, 'An Essay on the Civilisations of India, China and Japan' (n. 8), p. 87.

Conclusion: The Cambridge Trio and Posterity

The visionary proclamation of the Cambridge Trio that Chinese art is modern and accessible to Western audiences challenged the status quo, the legacy of which is palpable today. The Trio's scholarly contributions not only form part of the indispensable repertoire of Chinese art studies, but also influenced the fields of modern art, literature and social politics. Although the members' methodologies varied, their thought processes and analytical deductions were intimately intertwined from the early days of their friendship, blossoming with their shared passion for China and its culture while satisfying the criteria of modernist taste.

A formalist, Roger Fry was closest to a traditional art historian and critic. His aesthetics, applied to numerous categories of art, enabled him to see a continuity of emotion and spirit across the spectrum from the classical period to the modern, a parallel of which he discovered in ancient Chinese art. Devoid of context and meaning, his approach traversed hereto relatively unknown terrain, recognizing in the process its modernity. As Kenneth Clark wrote, 'in so far as taste can be changed by one man, it was changed by Roger Fry'.[354] Fry's method, however, should not be viewed as the antithesis of Arthur Waley's knowledge-oriented scholarship, but as its complement. While the unfamiliarity of Chinese art surrendered before formal interrogation, its inaccessibility disintegrated with Waley's transcription and contextual account in the most modern European manner. A meticulous linguist and sinologist, Waley bridged the cultural gap between Orient and Occident by presenting previously unapproachable indigenous material to both scholars and the wider public. It is questionable whether Fry and Waley's achievements would have received such recognition and reception had it not been for Goldsworthy Dickinson's tutorship, which extolled an idealized China as an alternative remedy for the West. Dickinson's societal perspective viewed the modernity of Chinese art as a manifestation of its

354 K. Clark, 'Introduction', in Fry, Last Lectures (n. 104), p. ix.

underlying institutional structure and belief system, the Western counterpart of which was found in the classical spirit of ancient Greek civilization. It would only be after internalizing these preconceptions of Chinese culture that Fry and Waley could fully communicate their visual and literary perspectives.

Although members of the Cambridge Trio made occasional errors in dating Chinese objects as well as regarding historical facts, these mistakes must be viewed in context. With contemporary Western knowledge of Chinese pictures described as akin to the 'dying Petrarch, clasping in his hand a Greek manuscript which he treasured though unable to read', and given the limited access to first-hand material, the insights reached by applying their methodological frameworks are remarkable.[355] With little precedent upon which to draw, the Trio was able to perform scholarly research of the highest calibre, with their approaches continuing to invigorate various liberal arts studies today. Whilst their conclusions were pioneering and set the stage for subsequent scholars, it is important also to cherish their methodologies and techniques as valuable tools for anthropocentric art historical research. As Roger Fry confessed in his letter to Goldsworthy Dickinson, it makes little difference 'at what periods things were made', rather it is the vitality of expression and clearness of idea that matter.[356]

The Trio's cultural impact on the reception of Chinese art is evidenced by the exhibition held at the Royal Academy of Arts in 1935, by which time Chinese art had entered 'so unobtrusively' into the daily life of the British audience.[357] Chinese 'objects' that had previously been destined for cabinets of curiosities began to

---

355 K. Clark, 'Introduction', in Fry, Last Lectures (n. 104), p. ix. Einstein, 'Some Notes on Chinese Painting' (n. 66), p. 185.

356 Fry, *Letters of Roger Fry* (n. 45), vol. II, p. 595.

357 *International Exhibition of Chinese Art,* Royal Academy of Arts, London, November 1935 – March 1936; L. Binyon, 'Introduction', *A Commemorative Catalogue of the International Exhibition of Chinese Art,* London 1936, pp. VII-VIII.

be recognized for their modernity and pioneering spirit. While Roger Fry saw the essence of Chinese art reappear in post-impressionism, challenging the Western canon, his formalist framework encouraged future scholars to apply similar techniques to other artistic movements. Arthur Waley's translations of Chinese poetry ceased to be the preserve of a small circle of specialists and became an integral part of Western heritage.[358] Goldsworthy Dickinson's analyses of ancient Chinese society and culture invigorated the intellectual establishment to increasingly include Chinese art in its writings of history. However, it was only a transitional period, rooted in the values of its time, moving towards a real historical assessment of Chinese art. As one strolls along the unrolled masterpieces of Chinese painting or admires Ming artefacts as emblems of cultural exchange, the Cambridge Trio triumphs and smiles, emanating from the late-night gatherings at King's College, annihilating time and space.

358 Morris, 'Arthur Waley' (n. 9), p. 50.

List of Illustrations

Fig. 1 – Roger Fry, *Goldsworthy Dickinson*, 1925, oil on canvas, 63.8 x 48.5 cm (King's College, Cambridge).

Fig. 2 – Roger Fry, *Self-Portrait*, 1918, oil on canvas, 79.8 x 59.3 cm (King's College, Cambridge).

Fig. 3 – Michael Ayrton, *Arthur Waley*, 1957, pencil on paper, 31.7 x 34.3 cm (King's College, Cambridge).

Fig. 4 – *Vase with Rudimentary Elephant-Head Handles*, 18th century, ceramic, 31.5 x 21.5 cm (The Courtauld Gallery, London).

Fig. 5 – A follower of Li Longmian, *A Sage in the Forest*, possibly Yuan dynasty (1271 – 1368), ink on paper, 26.0 x 32.0 cm. Present location unknown.

Fig. 6 – *You from Altar Stand*, Western Zhou dynasty (1046 – 771 BC), bronze, dimension unknown (The Metropolitan Museum of Art, New York).

Fig. 7 – *Wine Jar You*, late Shang dynasty (1600 – 1046 BC), bronze, 34.2 x 29.7 cm (Victoria and Albert Museum, London, formerly Eumorfopoulos collection).

Fig. 8 – After Zhang Zeduan, the bridge section of *Going up the River for the Spring Festival*, Southern Song dynasty (1127 – 1279), handscroll, ink and colour on silk, 29.2 x 624.8 cm (The British Museum, London).

Fig. 9 – After Zhang Zeduan, the wall section of *Going up the River for the Spring Festival*, Southern Song dynasty (1127 – 1279), handscroll, ink and colour on silk, 29.2 x 624.8 cm (The British Museum, London).

Fig. 10 – Attributed to Yan Liben, *The Drunken Daoist Monk*, Tang

dynasty (618 – 907), 33.0 x 80.0 cm (Collection of Adolphe Stoclet, Brussels).

Fig. 11 – Attributed to Li Longmian, *The Drunken Buddhist Monk*, Southern Song dynasty (1127 – 1279), handscroll, ink and colour on paper, 32.5 x 60.8 cm (Freer Gallery of Art, Washington, D.C.).

Fig. 12 – Yun Shouping (1633 – 1690), screen painted on silk, central portion, 1690 (Collection of Morton Sands).

Fig. 13 – *Jar in the Shape of an Owl*, Zhou dynasty (1046 – 256 BC), earthenware, 16.2 cm high (Musée Cernuschi, Paris).

Fig. 14 – *A Festive Scene*, Han dynasty (206 BC – AD 220), relief on brick and tile, 46.0 x 42.0 cm (Private collection, Chengdu).

Fig. 15 – *A Birdlike Creature with Human Face*, Han dynasty (206 BC – AD 220), relief on brick and tile, 31.0 x 40.5 cm (Private collection, Chengdu).

Fig. 16 – *Attempted Assassination*, Han dynasty (206 BC – AD 220), engraved stone (Musée Guimet, Paris).

Fig. 17 – *Two Heads* (from Hall of Zhu Wei, Jinxiang, Shandong), Han dynasty (206 BC – AD 220). Present location unknown.

Fig. 18 – Attributed to Guan Xiu, *Arhat*, The Five dynasties (907 – 960), 127.3 x 66.0 cm (Collection of Baron Takahashi, Tokyo).

Fig. 19 – *Taizong's Charger*, 649, limestone, 172.7 x 207.0 x 43.2 cm (University of Pennsylvania Museum of Archaeology and Anthropology, Philadelphia).

Fig. 20 – *Stone Sculpture of Bhikshu*, Tang dynasty (618 – 907). Present location unknown.

Fig. 21 – Italian sculptor influenced by Giotto, *The Art of Weaving*, mid-14th century, relief on Campanile, Florence.

Fig. 22 – *You*, late Shang dynasty (ca. 1550 – 1050 BC), bronze, 30.5 cm high (Collection of Baron Sumitomo, Tokyo).

Fig. 23 – *You Vessel in the Shape of a Feline*, late Shang dynasty (ca. 1550 – 1050 BC), bronze, 35.2 x 23.6 x 23.3 cm (Musée Cernuschi, Paris).

Fig. 24 – *Pou*, late Shang dynasty (12th – 11th century BC) (Collection of Takeuchi, Tokyo).

Fig. 25 – *Mirror*, Han dynasty (206 BC – AD 220), bronze, D. 17.8 cm.

Fig. 26 – *Mirror*, Han dynasty (206 BC – AD 220), bronze, D. 21.6 cm.

Fig. 27 – *Gilt-Bronze Garment Plaque*, 600 – 500 BC, China (Northern Hebei), 2.7 x 2.7 cm (The Courtauld Gallery, London).

Fig. 28 – *Bronze Pectoral Ornament in the Form of a Crouching Animal*, 600 – 500 BC, China (Northern Hebei), 4.5 cm long (The Courtauld Gallery, London).

Fig. 29 – *Guanyin*, Sui dynasty (590 – 618), stone, 88.9 cm high (Worchester Art Museum, MA).

Fig. 30 – *A Pair of Dancing Figures*, 20th century, ceramic (King's College, Cambridge, on loan to the Fitzwilliam Museum, Cambridge).

Fig. 31 – Muxi Fachang (1210 – 1269), *Returning Boats* (Count Matsudaira, Tokyo), and *A Fishing Village* (Collection of Nezu, Tokyo).

Fig. 32 – *The Fight for Buddha's Relics*, ca. 700, size unknown, wall painting from Dunhuang, cave 70.

Fig. 33 – After Wang Wei, *Clearing After Snowfall Along the River*, mid-16th century, handscroll, ink and colour on paper, 29.2 x 446.0 cm (Honolulu Museum of Art, HI, formerly Luo Zhenyu collection).

Fig. 34 –Attributed to Ma Yuan, *Boating by Moonlight*, Southern Song dynasty (1127 – 1279), hanging scroll, ink and colour on silk, 172.5 x 85.2 cm (The British Museum, London, formerly Eumorfopoulos collection).

Fig. 35 – Zhao Mengfu (1254 – 1322), *Two Horses*, 38.7 x 64.1 cm (Collection of Adolphe Stoclet, Brussels).

Fig. 36 – *Tripod Incense Burner*, Yuan dynasty (1279 – 1368), earthenware, 9.1 x 8.5 cm (The Courtauld Gallery, London).

Fig. 37 – *Tripod Pot*, Yangshao culture (5000 – 3000 BC) (Östasiatiska Museet, Stockholm).

Fig. 38 – *Bronze Tripod*, Zhou dynasty (1046 – 256 BC) (Calmann collection, Paris).

Fig. 39 – After Shi Ke, *The Second Patriarch in Contemplation*, 13th century, hanging scrolls, ink on paper, 35.3 x 64.4 cm (Tokyo National Museum, Tokyo).

Fig. 40 – Muxi Fachang (1210 – 1269), *Six Persimmons*, album leaf, ink on paper, 35.9 x 28.6 cm (Daitoku-ji, Kyoto).

Bibliography

Acker, William. *Some T'ang and Pre-T'ang Texts on Chinese Painting*, Leiden 1954.

Allan, Sarah. 'The *Taotie* Motif on Early Chinese Ritual Bronzes', in *The Zoomorphic Imagination in Chinese Art and Culture*, ed. Jerome Silbergeld and Eugene Wang, Honolulu 2016, pp. 21-66.

Anscombe, Isabelle. *Omega and After: Bloomsbury and the Decorative Arts*, London 1981.

Bachhofer, Ludwig. 'Chinese Landscape Painting in the Eighth Century', *The Burlington Magazine for Connoisseurs*, 67 (392), 1935, pp. 188-91.

Bagley, Robert. *Ancient Chinese Bronzes in the Arthur M. Sackler Collections, vol 1, Shang Ritual Bronzes in the Arthur M. Sackler Collections*, Washington, D.C. 1987.

Baker, Joan. *Hua Yu Lu (Dialogue on Painting)*, Guiling 2014.

Balfour, Ronald. 'Bibliography', in Edward Morgan Forster, *Goldsworthy Lowes Dickinson*, London 1934, pp. 244-68.

Barr, Alfred. Jr. *Matisse, his Art and his Public*, New York 1951.

Bell, Clive. *Art*, Dublin 1961.

Bell, Julian. *What is Painting? Representation and Modern Art*, Hong Kong 1999.

Bell, Quentin. *Bloomsbury*, London 1968.

Bell, Quentin. *Bloomsbury Recalled*, New York 1995.

Berenson, Bernard. *The Italian Painters of the Renaissance*, Oxford

1980.

Berger, Anton. *Josef Strzygowski: Von ihm und über ihn*, Graz 1923.

Bian, Zongshun, Zhou, Xu and Shi, Yuzhuo. *Zhongguo Gongyi Meishushi (History of Chinese Works of Art)*, Beijing 2008.

Binyon, Laurence. *The George Eumorfopoulos Collection: Catalogue of the Chinese Frescoes*, London 1927.

Binyon, Laurence. 'Chinese Painting', in *China Body & Soul*, ed. Ernest Hughes, London 1938.

Binyon, Laurence. 'Introduction', in *A Commemorative Catalogue of the International Exhibition of Chinese Art*, London 1936.

Binyon, Laurence. *Painting in the Far East: An Introduction to the History of Pictorial Art in Asia especially China and Japan*, London 1913.

Bishop, Charles. 'The Horses of T'ang T'ai-Tsung, of the Antecedents of the Chinese Horse', *The Museum Journal*, Philadelphia 1918, pp. 244-72.

British Museum. 'The Eumorfopoulos Collection', *The British Museum Quarterly*, 9 (3), 1935, pp. 86-8.

Bruneau, Anne. 'Fry, Roger Eliot', Oxford Dictionary of National Biography (website), 5, 2014.

Bullen, J. Barrie, ed. *The Post-Impressionists in England*, London and New York 1988.

Bunker, Emma. *Ancient Bronzes of the Eastern Eurasian Steppes from the Arthur M. Sackler Collection*, New York 1997.

Burling, Judith. and Burling, Arthur. *Chinese Art*, New York 1953.

Burlington Fine Arts Club, *Catalogue of a Collection of Objects of Chinese Art*, London 1915.

Bush, Susan. and Shih, Hsio-yen, ed. *Early Chinese Texts on Painting*, London 1985.

Bushell, Stephen. *Chinese Art*, London 1910.

Cahill, James. 'Confucian Elements in the Theory of Painting', in *The Confucian Persuasion*, ed. Arthur Wright, Stanford 1960, pp. 115-40.

Cahill, James. *Chinese Painting*, Cleveland 1960.

Cahill, James. 'Lecture 2 – Han Painting and Pictorial Designs', in *A Pure and Remote View: Visualizing Early Chinese Landscape Painting* (video).

Canfield, Cass. *The Incredible Pierpont Morgan*, New York 1974.

Catalogue of Works of Art in the Collection of King's College, Cambridge. Cambridge 1987.

Chavannes, Edouard. *La Sculpture sur pierre en Chine au temps des deux dynasties Han*, Paris 1893.

Cheng, J. Chester. 'Review of *The Opium War Through Chinese Eyes* by Arthur Waley', *Pacific Affairs*, 33 (1), 1960, pp. 68-9.

Clark, Kenneth. 'Introduction', in Roger Fry, *Last Lectures*, Cambridge 1939, pp. 9-29.

Cohn, William. *Chinese Painting*, London 1948.

Collingwood, Robin. *The Principles of Art*, London 1958.

Collins, Judith. *The Omega Workshops*, London 1983.

Contag, Victoria. 'The Unique Characteristics of Chinese Landscape Pictures', *Archives of the Chinese Art Society of America*, 6, 1952, pp. 45-63.

Contag, Victoria. *Zwei Meister chinesischer Landschaftsmalerei, Shih-t'ao und Shih-ch'i: Ein Beitrag zum Verständnis des Wesens chinesischer Landschaftsmalerei*, Baden-Baden 1955.

Corbett, David. *The Modernity of English Art 1914–30*, Manchester 1997.

Cork, Richard. *Art Beyond the Gallery in Early 20th Century England*, London 1985.

Courtauld Institute of Art. *Catalogue of the Fry Collection*, London 1958.

D'Allava, Anne. *Methods and Theories of Art History*, London 2005.

D'Ardenne de Tizac, Henri. *Animals in Chinese Art: A Collection of Examples*, London and Paris 1923.

David, Taylor. 'The Aesthetic Theories of Roger Fry Reconsidered', *Journal of Aesthetics*, 36, 1977, pp. 63-72.

De Bary, William. 'A Reappraisal of Neo-Confucianism', in *Studies in Chinese Thought*, ed. Arthur Wright, Chicago 1953, pp. 81-111.

De Gruchy, John. *Orienting Arthur Waley: Japonism, Orientalism, and the Creation of Japanese Literature in English*, Honolulu 2003.

Denis, Maurice. 'Cézanne', transl. Roger Fry, *The Burlington Magazine for Connoisseurs*, 16, 1910, pp. 207-19 and 275-80.

Dickinson, Goldsworthy. *Revolution and Reaction in Modern France*, London 1892.

Dickinson, Goldsworthy. 'The People as Humanity', in *Revolution and Reaction in Modern France*, London 1892, pp. 128-33.

Dickinson, Goldsworthy. *A Modern Symposium*, London 1905.

Dickinson, Goldsworthy. 'Eastern and Western Ideals: Being a Rejoinder to William Jennings Bryan', *Century Magazine*, 12, 1906, pp. 313-16.

Dickinson, Goldsworthy. *The Greek View of Life*, New York 1911.

Dickinson, Goldsworthy. *Religion and Immortality*, London 1911.

Dickinson, Goldsworthy. 'The Chances of the Chinese Republic', *Nation*, 6, 1913, pp. 491-2.

Dickinson, Goldsworthy. *The European Anarchy*, London 1916.

Dickinson, Goldsworthy. *The Choice Before Us*, London 1918.

Dickinson, Goldsworthy. 'The Seekers', The Papers of Goldsworthy Lowes Dickinson, King's College Archive, GLD/6/7A, 1929.

Dickinson, Goldsworthy. *Religion and Immortality*, London 1933.

Dickinson, Goldsworthy. *After Two Thousand Years: A Dialogue Between Plato and A Modern Young Man*, London 1930.

Dickinson, Goldsworthy. 'Letters from John Chinaman', *Letters from John Chinaman and Other Essays*, London 1946.

Dickinson, Goldsworthy. 'An Essay on the Civilisations of India, China and Japan', *Letters from John Chinaman and Other Essays*, London 1946.

Dickinson, Goldsworthy. 'The Contribution of Ancient Greece to Modern Life', *Letters from John Chinaman and Other Essays*,

London 1946.

Dickinson, Goldsworthy. *The Autobiography of G. Lowes Dickinson and Other Unpublished Writings*, ed. D. Proctor, London 1973.

Dickinson, Goldsworthy. 'Correspondence between Goldsworthy Lowes Dickinson and REF', The Papers of Roger Eliot Fry, King's College Archive, REF/3/46/1, 14 August 1988.

'Dickinson, Goldsworthy Lowes (DKN881GL)', ACAD – A Cambridge Alumni Database, University of Cambridge (website).

Dubosc, Jean. 'A New Approach to Chinese Painting', *Oriental Art*, 3 (2), 1950, pp. 55-57.

Ebrey, Patricia. and Bickford, Maggie. *Emperor Huizong and Late Northern Song China: The Politics of Culture and the Culture of Politics*, Cambridge, MA 2006.

Egbert, Donald. 'English Art Critics and Modern Social Radicalism', *Journal of Aesthetics*, 26, 1967, pp. 29-46.

Einstein, Lewis. 'Some Notes on Chinese Painting', *The Burlington Magazine for Connoisseurs*, 21 (112), 1912, pp. 185-87 and 190-92.

Elam, Caroline. *Roger Fry's Journey: From the Primitives to the Post-Impressionists*, Edinburgh 2008.

Elam, Caroline. 'From Giotto to the Bushmen: Roger Fry at the Slade 1909 – 13', *The Burlington Magazine*, 1386 (160), 2018, pp. 727-33.

Eliot, Thomas. *The Letters of T. S. Eliot. vol. I, 1898 – 1922*, ed. Valerie Eliot and Hugh Haughton, London 2009.

Elkins, James. *Chinese Landscape Painting as Western Art History*, London 2010.

Eskenazi Ltd. *Chinese Works of Art from the Stoclet Collection*. London 2003.

Fairbank, John. 'Review of *The Opium War through Chinese Eyes* by Arthur Waley', *Far Eastern Survey*, 28 (10), 1959, pp. 159-60.

Farr, Dennis. *English Art 1870 – 1940*, Oxford 1979.

Fenollosa, Ernest. *Epochs of Chinese and Japanese Art*, vol. II, London 1912.

Ferguson, John. *Outlines of Chinese Art*, Chicago 1919.

Ferguson, John. *Chinese Painting*, Chicago 1927.

Fischer, Otto. *Die Kunst Indiens, Chinas und Japans*, Berlin 1928.

Fischer, Otto. *Chinesische Landschaftsmalerei*, München 1921.

Fishman, Soloman. 'Roger Fry', in *The Interpretation of Art*, Berkeley and Los Angeles 1963.

Focillon, Henri. *The Life of Forms in Art*, New York 1948.

Fong, Wen. *Summer Mountains: The Timeless Landscape*, New York 1975.

Fong, Wen. *Beyond Representation: Chinese Painting and Calligraphy, 8th – 14th Century*, New York 1992.

Forster, Edward Morgan. 'Introduction', in *Letters from John Chinaman and Other Essays*, London 1946.

Forster, Edward Morgan. *Goldsworthy Lowes Dickinson*, London 1962.

Freer Gallery of Art. 'Object Documentation (F1968.18)', 2010.

Fried, Michael. 'Roger Fry's Formalism', *The Tanner Lectures on Human Values*, delivered at University of Michigan 2001.

Froula, Christine. 'War, Peace, and Internationalism', in *The Cambridge Companion to the Bloomsbury Group*, ed. Victoria Rosner, New York 2014, pp. 93-111.

Fry, Roger. *Giovanni Bellini*, London 1899.

Fry, Roger. 'Some Problems of Phenomenology and Its Application to Greek Painting: A Dissertation by R. E. Fry', The Papers of Roger Eliot Fry, King's College Archive, REF/1/13, 1891.

Fry, Roger. 'Chinese Art at the Whitechapel Gallery', *Athenaeum*, 3849, 1901, p. 165.

Fry, Roger. 'Introduction', in J. Reynolds, *Discourses*, London 1905, pp. 13-52.

Fry, Roger. 'The Chinese Exhibition', *Nation*, 1910, pp. 593-94.

Fry, Roger. 'Oriental Art', *Quarterly Review*, 212, 1910, pp. 212 and 225-39.

Fry, Roger. 'Review of *La philosophie de la nature dans l'art d'Extrême-Orient* by Raphael Petrucci', *The Burlington Magazine for Connoisseurs*, 19, 1911, pp. 106-7.

Fry, Roger. 'Richard Bennet Collection of Chinese Porcelain', *The Burlington Magazine for Connoisseurs*, 19, 1911, pp. 133-37.

Fry, Roger. 'Review of Ruins of Desert Cathay by M. A. Stein', *The Burlington Magazine for Connoisseurs*, 21, 1912, p. 174.

Fry, Roger. 'Children's Drawings', *The Burlington Magazine for Connoisseurs*, 30 (171), 1917, pp. 225-27 and 231.

Fry, Roger. 'Drawing or Design', The Papers of Roger Eliot Fry, King's College Archive, REF/1/131, 1920 – 1929.

Fry, Roger. 'A Toad in White Jade', *The Burlington Magazine for Connoisseurs*, 41 (234), 1922, p. 103.

Fry, Roger. 'An Essay in Aesthetics', *Vision and Design*, London, 1923, pp. 16-38.

Fry, Roger. 'Introduction', in H. d'Ardenne de Tizac, *Animals in Chinese Art: A Collection of Examples*, London and Paris 1923.

Fry, Roger. 'Some Chinese Antiquities', *The Burlington Magazine for Connoisseurs*, 43 (249), 1923, pp. 276-81.

Fry, Roger. 'Oriental Art. Review of *An Introduction to the Study of Chinese Painting* by Arthur Waley', *The Burlington Magazine for Connoisseurs*, 44, 1924, pp. 47-48.

Fry, Roger. 'Review of *The Year-Book of Oriental Art and Culture 1924 – 1925* Edited by Arthur Waley', *Nation and Athenaeum*, 1925, p. 650.

Fry, Roger. 'Chinese Art', *Burlington Magazine Monographs*, London, 1925, pp. 5-12.

Fry, Roger. Unpublished letter to Raymond Henniker-Heaton, object archive 1925. 118, 1925, Worcester Art Museum, MA.

Fry, Roger. 'Chinese Bronzes at Messrs. Yamanaka's', *Nation and Athenaeum*, 1926, pp. 494-95.

Fry, Roger. 'Chinese Frescoes', *Nation and Athenaeum*, 1927, pp. 751-52.

Fry, Roger. 'The Eumorfopoulos Collection', *Nation and Athenaeum*, 1928, pp. 652-53.

Fry, Roger. *Henri Matisse*, London and Paris 1930.

Fry, Roger. 'Scythian and Chinese', *The Arts of Painting and Sculpture*, London 1932, pp. 65-80.

Fry, Roger. 'A Memoir', *Goldsworthy Lowes Dickinson, 6 August 1862, 3 August 1932: Fellow of the College, 1887 – 1932*, Cambridge 1933, pp. 5-17.

Fry, Roger. 'Review of *A History of Early Chinese Painting* by Osvald Sirén', *The New Statesman and Nation*, 1933, p. 17.

Fry, Roger. 'Chinese Art and Architecture', in *China Body & Soul*, ed. Ernest Hughes,London 1938, pp. 27-43.

Fry, Roger. *Last Lectures*, Cambridge 1939.

Fry, Roger. 'Reflections on British Painting', in *French, Flemish and British Art*, London 1951, pp. 137-212.

Fry, Roger. 'Characteristics of French Art', in *French, Flemish and British Art*, London 1951, pp. 3-96.

Fry, Roger. 'Some Questions in Esthetics', in *Transformations*, New York 1968, pp. 1-43.

Fry, Roger. 'Some Aspects of Chinese Art', in *Transformations*, New York 1968, pp. 67-81.

Fry, Roger. *Letters of Roger Fry*, ed. Denys Sutton, London 1972.

Fry, Roger. 'Retrospect', in *Vision and Design*, London 1981.

Fry, Roger. 'Giotto', in *Vision and Design*, London 1981.

Fry, Roger. 'Paul Cézanne', in *Vision and Design*, London 1981.

Fry, Roger. 'The French Post-Impressionists', in *Vision and Design*,

London 1981.

Fry, Roger. *Cézanne: A Study of His Development*, Chicago and London 1989.

Fry, Roger. 'Correspondence between Goldsworthy Lowes Dickinson and REF', The Papers of Roger Eliot Fry, King's College Archive, REF/3/46/2, 23 June 1989.

Fry, Roger. 'Children's Drawings', The Papers of Roger Eliot Fry, King's College Archive, REF/1/23.

Fry, Roger. 'I. Transition from Classical to Modern Art', The Papers of Roger Eliot Fry, King's College Archive, REF/1/65/1.

Fry, Roger. 'Review of Chinese Porcelain and Hard Stones by E. Gorer and J. F. Blacker', The Papers of Roger Eliot Fry, King's College Archive, REF/1/19.

'George Aristedes Eumorfopoulos 1863 – 1939 Collector, Businessman, and Philanthropist', *The Smithsonian's Museums of Asian Art*, 2016.

Giles, Herbert. *A Chinese Biographical Dictionary*, London 1898.

Giles, Herbert. *A History of Chinese Literature*, London 1901.

Giles, Herbert. *An Introduction to the History of Chinese Pictorial Art*, London 1918.

Gombrich, Ernst. *The Preference for the Primitive: Episodes in the History of Western Taste and Art*, London 2002.

Goodman, Charles. 'Arthur Waley Remembered', *The Charleston Magazine*, 6, 1992 – 1993, pp. 5-8.

Graham, Jenny. 'A Note on the Early Reputation of Roger Fry', *The Burlington Magazine*, 143 (1181), 2001, pp. 493-99.

Gray, Basil. 'The Development of Taste in Chinese Art in the West 1872 – 1972', *Studies in Chinese and Islamic Art, vol. I Chinese Art*, London 1985, pp. 17-23. Originally published in *Transactions of the Oriental Ceramic Society*, 39, 1971 – 1973, pp. 19-41.

Gray, Basil. 'Waley, Arthur David', rev. Glen Dudbridge, Oxford Dictionary of National Biography (website).

Green, Christopher. 'Into the Twentieth Century: Roger Fry's Project Seen from 2000', in *Art Made Modern: Roger Fry's Vision of Art*, ed. Christopher Green, London 2000, pp. 13-30.

Green, Christopher. 'Roger Fry's Canon', in *Art Made Modern*, ed. Christopher Green, London 2000, pp. 135-212.

Greenberg, Clement. 'Avant-Garde and Kitsch', in *Art and Culture: Critical Essays*, Boston 1967, pp. 3-21.

Grousset, René. *Les civilisations de l'Orient*, Paris 1929 – 1930.

Grousset, René. *L'art de l'Extrême Orient: paysages, fleurs, animaux: 15 planches en couleurs d'après les tableaux des vieux maîtres chinois et japonais*, Paris 1936.

Hannay, Howard. *Roger Fry and Other Essays*, London 1937.

Hardie, Peter. 'Ferdinand Schiller, Collecting Chinese Art 1913 – 1936', *Journal of Museum Ethnography*, 15, 2003, pp. 35-46.

Harding, Jason. 'Goldsworthy Lowes Dickinson and the King's College Mandarins', *The Cambridge Quarterly*, 2011, pp. 26-42.

Harrison, Charles. 'Roger Fry in Retrospect', *Studio International*, 171, 1966, p. 220-21.

Harrison, Charles. *English Art and Modernism, 1900 – 39*, New Haven 1981.

Hennessy, John. 'Roger Fry and the Metropolitan Museum', in *Oxford, China and Italy: Writings in Honour of Sir Harold Acton*, ed. Edward Chaney and Neil Ritchie, London 1984, pp. 229-40.

Hobson, Robert. *Chinese Art. One Hundred Plates in Colour. Introduced by an Outline Sketch of Chinese Art*, London 1927.

Homberger, Eric, ed. *The Cambridge Mind: Ninety Years of the Cambridge Review, 1879 – 1969*, London 1970.

House, John, et al. *Impressionism for England: Samuel Courtauld as Patron and Collector*, exhibition catalogue, The Courtauld Gallery, London 1994.

Huang, Michelle. 'British Interest in Chinese Painting, 1881 – 1910', *Journal of the History of Collections*, 22, 2010, pp. 279-87.

Huang, Michelle. 'Laurence Binyon: A Pioneering and Authoritative Curator of Chinese Painting in Early Twentieth-Century Britain', *Museum History Journal*, 8 (1), 2015, pp. 41-58.

'Introduction', *The Tradition of Re-Presenting in Art: Originality and Reproduction in Chinese Painting and Calligraphy*, National Palace Museum (website), 2008.

Jenyns, Soame. *A Background to Chinese Painting*, London 1935.

Johns, Francis. *A Bibliography of Arthur Waley*, London 1968.

Johns, Francis. 'Bibliography: Introducing the East', 1968, The Papers of Arthur David Waley, King's College Archive, ADW/4/5.

Karetzky, Patricia. *Court Art of the Tang*, London 1996.

Kerr, Douglas. and Kuehn, Julia. ed. *A Century of Travels in China: Critical Essays on Travel Writing from the 1840s to the 1940s*, Hong Kong 2007.

Krauss, Rosalind. 'In the Name of Picasso', *The Originality of the Avant-Garde and Other Modernist Myths*, London 1985, pp. 5-22.

Krauss, Rosalind. *The Picasso Papers*, Cambridge, MA 1999.

Kuo, Jisheng. *Yishu Shi yu Yishu Piping (Art History and Criticism)*, Taipei 2007.

Kümmel, Otto. *Die Kunst Ostasiens*, Berlin 1921.

Kümmel, Otto. *Ausstellung chinesischer Kunst: Veranstaltet von der Gesellschaft für Ostasiatische Kunst und der Preussischen Akademie der Künste*, Berlin 1929.

Laing, Donald. *Roger Fry: An Annotated Bibliography of the Published Writings*, New York and London 1979.

Laurence, Patricia. *Lily Briscoe's Chinese Eyes: Bloomsbury, Modernism, and China*, Columbia, SC 2003.

Ledderose, Lothar. 'Kunstgeschichte und Weltkunstgeschichte', *Saeculun*, 40 (2), 1989, pp. 136-41.

Lee, Sherman. 'The Story of Chinese Painting', *Art Quarterly*, 4, 1948, pp. 9-31.

Lee, Sherman. *Chinese Landscape Painting*, Cleveland 1962.

Lee, Sherman. and Fong, Wen. *Streams and Mountains Without End: A Northern Sung Handscroll and its Significance in the History of Early Chinese Painting*, Ascona 1955.

Lei, Ziren. *Ren Ji Yu Shan: Ming Dai Shanshui Hua Jing Zhong de Renwu, Jiegou yu Zhiqu (Traces of Human Presence in Mountains: Human Figures, Composition and Significance of Chinese Landscape Painting in 14th – 17th Century)*, Beijing 2010.

Li, Zhouliang. 'Taolun Qian Zhongshu "Liufa" Shidu Shuo'

('Discussion on Qian Zhongshu's "Six Principles" and Lost Meanings'), *Xueshu Jiaoliu (Academic Exchange)*, 4 (109), 2003.

Lin, Hsiu-ling. 'Reconciling Bloomsbury's Aesthetics of Formalism with the Politics of Anti-Imperialism: Roger Fry's and Clive Bell's Interpretation of Chinese Art', *Concentric: Studies in English Literature and Linguistics*, 27. 1, 2001, pp. 151-89.

Lin, Yutang. transl. *The Chinese Theory of Art*, London 1967.

Llewellyn, William. 'Preface', *Catalogue of the International Exhibition of Chinese Art 1935 – 6*, London 1936, pp. 4-5.

Lubenow, William. *The Cambridge Apostles, 1820 – 1914: Liberalism, Imagination, and Friendship in British Intellectual and Professional Life*, Cambridge 1998.

Lü, Buwei. *Lüshi Chunqiu (Discourse of Lü Buwei)*.

Lü, Dalin. *Kao Gu Tu (Archaeology Icon)*.

Lü, Peng. *Xi Shan Qing Yuan: Liang Song Shiqi Shanshui Hua de Lishi yu Qüwei Zhuanxing (Pure Views: Remote from Streams and Mountains: Chinese Landscape Painting in 10th – 13th Century)*, Beijing 2004.

Marcus, Laura. 'Bloomsbury Aesthetics', in *The Cambridge Companion to the Bloomsbury Group*, ed. Victoria Rosner, New York 2014, pp. 162-80.

McDowell, Frederick. 'E. M. Forster and Goldsworthy Lowes Dickinson', *Studies in the Novel*, 5 (4), 1973, pp. 441-56.

Melman, Billie. 'Under the Western Historian's Eyes: Eileen Power and the Early Feminist Encounter with Colonialism', *History Workshop Journal*, 42, 1996, pp. 147-68.

Molesworth, Charles. *The Capitalist and the Critic: J.P. Morgan, Roger Fry, and the Metropolitan Museum of Art*, Austin 2016.

Morphet, Richard. 'Roger Fry: The Nature of His Painting', *The Burlington Magazine*, 122, 1980, pp. 462, 478 and 481-89.

Morris, Ivan. 'Arthur Waley', *Encounter*, 12, 1966, pp. 50-57.

Morris, Ivan, ed. 'Arthur Waley in Conversation', *Madly Singing in the Mountains: An Appreciation and Anthology of Arthur Waley*, London 1970, pp. 138-51.

Nakata, Yujirō. and Fu, Shen. ed. *Ōbei shuzō: Chūgoku hōsho meisekishū (Masterpieces of Chinese Calligraphy in American and European Collections)*, vol. I, Tokyo 1981.

'Newscuttings and Letter', *The Morning Post*, January 1918, The Papers of Goldsworthy Lowes Dickinson, King's College Archive, GLD/6/4.

Nylan, Michael. 'Arthur Waley and Li Zehou: Two Aesthetes Translating', *Art in Translation*, 5, 2013, pp. 165-82.

'Obituary', *The Cambridge Review*, October 14, 1932, The Papers of Goldsworthy Lowes Dickinson, King's College Archive, GLD/6/9.

'Obituary', *The Times*, August 4, 1932, The Papers of Goldsworthy Lowes Dickinson, King's College Archive, GLD/6/9.

Ouyang, Xiu. and Song, Qi. *Xin Tang Shu (New Tang History).*

Pelliot, Paul. *Les grottes de Touen-Houang: peintures et sculptures bouddhiques des époques des Wei, des T'ang et des Song, tome second, grottes 31 à 72*, Paris 1920.

Petrucci, Raphael. *La philosophie de la nature dans l'art d'Extrême-Orient*, Paris 1910.

Petrucci, Raphael. *Les peintres chinois*, Paris 1912.

Pierson, Stacey, ed. *Collecting Chinese Art: Interpretation and Display*, London 2000.

Pierson, Stacey. 'From Market and Exhibition to University: Sir Percival David and the Institutionalization of Chinese Art History in England', in *Collecting China: The World, China, and a History of Collecting*, ed. V. Rujivacharakul, Plymouth 2011.

Qian, Zhongshu. *Guan Zhui Bian (Limited Views: Essays on Ideas and Letters)*, Beijing 1979.

Qin, Xuanfu. 'Read: How to Look at Chinese Painting', CAFA Art Info (website) 2016.

Rackham, Bernard. 'Review of *The Chinese Exhibition: A Commemorative Catalogue of the International Exhibition of Chinese Art* by Laurence Binyon', *The Burlington Magazine for Connoisseurs*, 70 (407), 1937, p. 95.

Rawson, Jessica. *Ancient China: Art and Archaeology*, London 1980.

Rawson, Jessica. *The British Museum Book of Chinese Art*, London 2007.

Reed, Christopher. 'The Fry Collection at the Courtauld Institute Galleries', *The Burlington Magazine*, 132 (1052), 1990.

Reed, Christopher. *A Roger Fry Reader*, Chicago and London 1996.

Reed, Christopher. 'A Room of One's Own: The Bloomsbury Group's Creation of a Modernist Domesticity', in *Not at Home. The Suppression of Domesticity in Modern Art and Architecture*, London 1996, pp.147-60.

Reed, Christopher. 'Roger Fry: The Art of Bloomsbury. San Marino and London', *The Burlington Magazine*, 142 (1165), 2000, pp. 262-65.

Richards, Ivor. 'The Chinese Renaissance', *Scrutiny*, 9, 1932, pp. 102-13.

Roberts, Laurence. *The Bernard Berenson Collection of Oriental Art at Villa I Tatti*, New York 1991.

Rosner, Victoria. 'Introduction', in T*he Cambridge Companion to the Bloomsbury Group*, ed. Victoria Rosner, New York 2014, pp. 1-16.

Rudolph, Richard. and Wen, Yu. ed. *Han Tomb Art of West China: A Collection of First- and Second-Century Reliefs*, Berkeley and Los Angeles 1951.

Russell, Bertrand. *The Problem of China*, London 1922.

Santori, Flaminia. 'European "Masterpieces" for America: Roger Fry and the Metropolitan Museum of Art', in *Art Made Modern*, ed. Christopher Green, London 2000, pp. 107-18.

Shelton, Anthony, ed. *Collectors: Individuals and Institutions*, London 2001.

Shi Qü Bao Ji (Precious Book Box of the Stone Drain), Shanghai 1918.

Shiff, Richard. 'Painting, Writing, Handwriting', in R. Fry, *Cézanne: A Study of His Development*, Chicago and London 1989, pp. 10-28.

Sickman, Laurence. and Shone, Richard. *Bloomsbury Portraits: Vanessa Bell, Duncan Grant and Their Circle*, London 1976.

Simon, Eugène. *La cité chinoise*, Paris 1885.

Sirén, Osvald. *Histoire des arts anciens de la Chine*, vol. II, Paris and Brussels 1929.

Sirén, Osvald. *A History of Early Chinese Painting*, vol. I, London 1933.

Soper, Alexander. 'Early Chinese Landscape Painting', *The Art Bulletin*, 23 (2), 1941, pp. 141-64.

Soper, Alexander. 'Life-Motion and the Sense of Space in Early Chinese Representational Art', *The Art Bulletin*, 30 (3), 1948, pp. 167-86.

Soper, Alexander. *The Art and Architecture of China*, Baltimore 1968.

Sorensen, Lee, ed. 'Fry, Roger', Dictionary of Art Historians (website).

Soulier, Gustave. *Les influences orientales dans la peinture toscane*, Paris 1924.

Spalding, Frances. *Roger Fry: Art and Life*, Berkeley 1980.

Spalding, Frances. 'Roger Fry and His Critics in a Post-Modernist Age', *The Burlington Magazine*, 128 (1000), 1986, pp. 489-92.

Speiser, Werner. *China Spirit and Society*, London 1960.

Stair, Julian. 'The Employment of Matter: Pottery of the Omega Workshop', in *Beyond Bloomsbury: Designs of the Omega Workshops 1913 – 19*, ed. Alexandra Gerstein, London 2009, pp. 27-33.

Stein, Aurel. *Guide to an Exhibition of Paintings, Manuscripts, and Other Archaeological Objects Collected by Sir Aurel Stein in Chinese Turkestan*, London 1914.

Sullivan, Michael. 'On the Origin of Landscape Representation in Chinese Art', *Archives of the Chinese Art Society of America*, 7, 1953, pp. 54-65.

Sullivan, Michael. 'Pictorial Art and the Attitude Toward Nature in Ancient China', *The Art Bulletin*, 36 (1), 1954, pp. 1-19.

Sullivan, Michael. *The Meeting of Eastern and Western Art*, London

1989.

Summers, David. 'Heinrich Wölfflin's "Kunstgeschichtliche Grundbegriffe", 1915', *The Burlington Magazine*, 151 (1276), 2009, pp. 476-79.

Suzuki, Gei. 'Li Gonglin', *Zhong Guo Hui Hua Shi (Chinese Painting History)*, vol. I, transl. M. Wei, Taipei 1987.

The British Museum. *Ming: 50 Years that Changed China*, London 2014.

The Home House Trustees. *Catalogue of the Pictures and other Works of Art at Home House*, London 1935.

The Fitzwilliam Museum. *Cambridge Portraits: From Lely to Hockney*, Cambridge 1978.

Thorp, Rober. *China in the Early Bronze Age: Shang Civilization*, Philadelphia 2005.

Tolstoy, Lev. *What is Art?*, transl. Aylmer Maude, 1899.

Tomlinson, Charles. 'Introduction', *The Oxford Book of Verse in English Translation*, Oxford 1980.

Tong, Qingsheng. 'Towards a Common Civilization: G. Lowes Dickinson, China, and Global Humanism', *Canadian Review of Comparative Literature*, 6, 2014, pp. 156-73.

Umehara, Sueji. ed. *The Collection of Old Bronzes of Sumitomo*, Kyoto 1971.

Victoria and Albert Museum. *Chinese Art: The Eumorfopoulos Collection*, London 1936.

Virgin, Louise. and Abe, Stanley. Communication, 2010 – 2011, Worcester Art Museum, MA.

Waley, Arthur. 'A Chinese Picture', *The Burlington Magazine for Connoisseurs*, 30 (166), 1917, pp. 3-10.

Waley, Arthur. 'The Rarity of Ancient Chinese Paintings', *The Burlington Magazine for Connoisseurs*, 30 (171), 1917, pp. 209-14.

Waley, Arthur. 'A Chinese Portrait', *The Burlington Magazine for Connoisseurs*, 31 (175), 1917, p. 131.

Waley, Arthur. 'Further Poems by Po Chu-I', The Papers of Arthur David Waley, King's College Archive, ADW/4/2, undated (after 1918).

Waley, Arthur. 'To the Bachelor-of-Arts P'ei Ti', *Reconstruction*, 1 (9), 1918.

Waley, Arthur. 'Recent Acquisitions for Public Collections – VII. A Sketch from Tun-Huang-British Museum, Print Room, Stein Collection', *The Burlington Magazine for Connoisseurs*, 34 (191), 1919, p. 55.

Waley, Arthur. 'A Painting by Yen Li-Pen', *The Burlington Magazine for Connoisseurs*, 35 (200), 1919, p. 198.

Waley, Arthur. 'Note on the Invention of Woodcuts', *The New China Review*, 1 (4), 1919, pp. 412-15.

Waley, Arthur. 'Chinese Philosophy of Art – I. Note on the "Six Methods"', *The Burlington Magazine for Connoisseurs*, 37, 1920, pp. 309-10.

Waley, Arthur. 'Chinese Philosophy of Art – II. Wang Wei and Chang Yen-Yüan', *The Burlington Magazine for Connoisseurs*, 38, 1921, p. 32.

Waley, Arthur. 'Chinese Philosophy of Art – III. Ching Hao', *The Burlington Magazine for Connoisseurs*, 38 (216), 1921, pp. 111-12.

Waley, Arthur. 'Chinese Philosophy of Art – IV. Kuo His (Part I)', *The Burlington Magazine for Connoisseurs*, 38 (218), 1921, p. 244.

Waley, Arthur. 'Chinese Philosophy of Art – V. Kuo His (Part II)', *The Burlington Magazine for Connoisseurs*, 39 (220), 1921, pp. 10-11.

Waley, Arthur. 'Chinese Philosophy of Art – VI', *The Burlington Magazine for Connoisseurs*, 39 (221), 1921, p. 84.

Waley, Arthur. 'Chinese Philosophy of Art – VII. Tung Ch'i-ch'ang (1)', *The Burlington Magazine for Connoisseurs*, 39 (222), 1921, p. 128.

Waley, Arthur. 'Chinese Philosophy of Art – VIII', *The Burlington Magazine for Connoisseurs*, 39 (224), 1921, pp. 235-6.

Waley, Arthur. 'Chinese Philosophy of Art – IX. (Concluded)', *The Burlington Magazine for Connoisseurs*, 39 (225), 1921, p. 292.

Waley, Arthur. 'An Introspective Romance', *The New Statesman*, 12, 1921, pp. 286-7.

Waley, Arthur. *Zen Buddhism and Its Relation to Art*, London 1922.

Waley, Arthur. 'Ricci and Tung Ch'i-Ch'ang', *Bulletin of the School of Oriental and African Studies*, 2 (2), 1922, pp. 342-3.

Waley, Arthur. *An Index of Chinese Artists Represented in the Sub-Department of Oriental Prints and Drawings in the British Museum*, London 1922.

Waley, Arthur. 'Chinese Temple Paintings', *The Burlington Magazine for Connoisseurs*, 41 (236), 1922, p. 228.

Waley, Arthur. 'On the Criticism, Collection, Purchase and Handling of Pictures', *Asia Major*, 1923.

Waley, Arthur. 'Animals in Chinese Art', *The Burlington Magazine for Connoisseurs*, 42 (242), 1923, pp. 215-16.

Waley, Arthur. 'T'ai Tsung's Six Chargers', *The Burlington Magazine for Connoisseurs*, 43, 1923, pp. 117-18.

Waley, Arthur. transl. and ed. 'The Tsun Sheng Pa Chien, A.D. 1591 by Kao Lien', *The Year Book of Oriental Art and Culture 1924 – 1925*, London, 1925.

Waley, Arthur. 'Yün Shou-P'ing Called "Nan-T'ien", 1633 – 1690', *The Year Book of Oriental Art and Culture 1924 – 1925*, London, 1925.

Waley, Arthur. and Yetts, Walter. 'The T'ao-t'ieh', *The Burlington Magazine for Connoisseurs*, 48 (275), 1926, p. 104.

Waley, Arthur. *A Catalogue of Paintings Recovered from Tun-Huang by Sir Aurel Stein, K. C. I. E.*, London 1931.

Waley, Arthur. *The Way and Its Power: A Study of the Tao Tê Ching and Its Place in Chinese Thought*, London 1934.

Waley, Arthur. *The Analects of Confucius*, London 1938.

Waley, Arthur. 'Our Debt to China', *The Asiatic Review*, 7, 1940, pp. 554-57.

Waley, Arthur. 'Roger Fry', *The Listener*, 8, 1940, p. 243.

Waley, Arthur. 'Intellectual Conversation', *Abinger Chronicle*, 4, 1943, pp. 34-37, The Papers of Arthur David Waley, King's College Archive, ADW/4/3.

Waley, Arthur. 'Life Under the Han Dynasty', *History Today*, 1953, pp. 89-98.

Waley, Arthur. *An Introduction to the Study of Chinese Painting*, London 1958 (First published 1923).

Waley, Arthur. *The Opium War Through Chinese Eyes*, London 1958.

Waley, Arthur. *A Hundred and Seventy Chinese Poems*, London 1962.

Waley, Arthur. *The Secret History of the Mongols*, London 1964.

Waley, Arthur. *A Half of Two Lives*, London 1982.

Waley, Daniel. 'Arthur Waley: A Memoir', 2001, The Papers of Arthur David Waley, King's College Archive, ADW/1/6.

Waley, Margaret. 'Identifications. Persons to whom copies of poems (1916) were to be given', The Papers of Arthur David Waley, King's College Archive, ADW/1/4, pp. 1-18.

Waley, Margaret. 'Manuscript Memoir of Arthur Waley', The Papers of Arthur David Waley, King's College Archive, ADW/1/1.

Walravens, Hartmut. *Bibliographien zur ostasiatischen Kunstgeschichte in Deutschland*, Hamburg 1984.

Wang, Daisy. 'C. T. Loo and the Chinese Art Collection at the Freer, 1915 – 1951', *Arts of Asia*, 41, 2011, pp. 104-16.

Wang, Shixiang. *Zhongguo Hualun Yanjiu (Study on Chinese Painting Theory)*, vol. I, Beijing 2014.

Watney, Simon. 'The Connoisseur as Gourmet: The Aesthetics of Roger Fry and Clive Bell', in ed. Tony Bennett, *Formations of Pleasure*, London 1983, pp. 66-83.

Watson, Ftancis. 'He Never Went to China – A Portrait of Arthur Waley', *The Listener 2 August 1979*, compiled and presented for Radio 3, King's College Archive, ADW 4/4.

Woolf, Virginia. *Roger Fry: A Biography*, London 1969.

Wu, Hung. *The Wu Liang Shrine: The Ideology of Early Chinese Pictorial Art*, Stanford 1989.

Wu, Hung. *Monumentality in Early Chinese Art and Architecture*, Stanford 1995.

Xu, Beihong. 'The Paris Chinese Art Exhibition: Brilliance of Antique Paintings', *Art Theory of Beihong*, 1933, Nanjing library (website).

Yetts, Walter. 'Bronzes', *Burlington Magazine Monographs*, London 1925, pp. 31-46.

Yeats, William. 'Introduction', *The Oxford Book of Modern Verse*, Oxford 1936, pp. 5-13.

'You Vessels in the Shape of a Feline', *Musée Cernuschi* (website).

Zhang, Yanyuan. *Li Dai Ming Hua Ji (Famous Paintings Through History)*, ed. Jianhua Yü, Shanghai 1964.

Zhou, Xiuqin. 'The Mausoleum of Emperor Tang Taizong', *Sino-Platonic Papers*, 187, 2009, pp. 1-380.

Zong, Bin. 'Hua Shan Shui Xu' ('Preface to Landscape Painting'), transl. Yütang Lin, in *The Chinese Theory of Art*, London 1967.

Zuo, Qiuming. 'Wen Gong Shi Ba Nian', *Zuo Zhuan* ('The Eighteenth Year of Weng Gong', *Commentary of Zuo*).

Printed in Great Britain
by Amazon

39693742R00096